Marian Cox

Cambridge IGCSE®
First
Language
English

Language and Skills Practice Book

Fifth edition

CAMBRIDGE
UNIVERSITY PRESS

CAMBRIDGE
UNIVERSITY PRESS

Shaftesbury Road, Cambridge CB2 8EA, United Kingdom

One Liberty Plaza, 20th Floor, New York, NY 10006, USA

477 Williamstown Road, Port Melbourne, VIC 3207, Australia

314–321, 3rd Floor, Plot 3, Splendor Forum, Jasola District Centre,
New Delhi – 110025, India

103 Penang Road, #05-06/07, Visioncrest Commercial, Singapore 238467

Cambridge University Press is part of the University of Cambridge.

It furthers the University's mission by disseminating knowledge in the pursuit of
education, learning and research at the highest international levels of excellence.

www.cambridge.org
Information on this title: www.cambridge.org/9781108438926

First published 2003
Third edition 2010
Fourth edition 2014
Fifth edition 2018

20 19 18 17 16 15

Printed in the Netherlands by Wilco BV

ISBN 978-1-108-43892-6 Paperback

A catalogue record for this publication is available from the British Library

Introduction

This Practice Book forms part of the suite of Cambridge IGCSE® First Language English Coursebook resources authored by Marian Cox including the Coursebook, Teacher's Resource and English Exam Preparation and Practice book[1], all by Cambridge University Press. The skills offered for practice are those used in the Cambridge IGCSE and IGCSE (9–1) First Language English syllabuses. These skills and approaches are a continuation and development of those included in the Cambridge Lower Secondary curriculum framework.

The Practice Book is a standalone resource that forms a follow-on component from the Coursebook. It is particularly designed for students seeking additional practice after the completion of the course and prior to assessment. In addition, it can be used as a dip-in resource containing extension activities that teachers can direct students towards in order to further practice topics covered in the Coursebook. Alternatively, it can be used in parallel to the Coursebook to provide less confident students the opportunity to focus on particular areas needing specific skills practice.

This Practice Book contains 12 independent units, each based on a different topic, containing two or three themed texts, and divided into the sections Language and Style, Comprehension and Summary, Directed Writing, and Composition. Each unit gives practice in the response techniques of skimming, scanning, selecting, collating and structuring. The topics have been selected to cater for a variety of interests and to have international appeal to the relevant age group. The passages cover the range of genres for Reading and Writing tasks. They give further opportunities to practise the Reading and Writing skills and language points that are introduced or revisited in the Coursebook, or made the focus of the lesson plans provided in the Teacher Resource.

The units are roughly equal in level of difficulty and can be studied in any order. Each unit contains a mixture of assessment tasks for skills practice as well as specific language exercises on spelling, punctuation, vocabulary extension or grammar points. There is a supplementary grammar and punctuation reference section at the end of the Practice Book which defines and explains the language points referred to in the book. Teachers can select tasks according to which skills and language areas need practising at a particular time by a particular student or class. The Contents indicate which language areas and assessment tasks are contained in each unit.

Every unit gives practice in summary and explaining writers' effects. The Directed Writing tasks give opportunities to practise the prescribed range of response genres: letter, report, article, journal, speech, interview and summary. The descriptive and narrative composition choices at the end of each unit are scaffolded to help with planning and structure.

By using this Practice Book, students will become familiar with a range of assessment passages and tasks, and gain practice in writing in different voices and styles for different audiences and purposes. The tasks can be done in class, as homework (differentiated if desired), or by the student working independently. An Answers appendix gives suggested answers for tasks where appropriate, though these are not necessarily definitive. (The appendix can be removed from student copies of the workbook.) Answer space for all questions is provided in the Practice Book, the size of the space indicating the required length of the response.

iii

---

[1] This text has not been through the Cambridge International endorsement process.

Contents

	Reading skills	Writing skills	Reading text type	Writing text type	Grammar	Punctuation
Unit 1: Rocket science			Letter Encyclopedia article	News report Blog post	Prefixes Parts of speech Passive voice Quantifiers	
Unit 2: Bear essentials	Writers' effects		Article Short story Fact box	Magazine article Speech	Prefixes	Parentheses Dashes and hyphens Commas
Unit 3: Simply flying		Spelling	Article Advertisement	Interview Job application letter	Prefixes	Dashes and hyphens
Unit 4: On the ball		Spelling	Article	Dialogue Evaluative letter	Prefixes Parts of speech	Apostrophes Semi-colons Dialogue
Unit 5: Great rivers	Fact v. opinion Writers' effect	Sentence structures	Article Novel	Dialogue Complaint letter	Parts of speech Complex sentences	Commas
Unit 6: Elephant tales		Synonyms	Article Fable	News report Journal	Prefixes	Dialogue
Unit 7: Bricks and stones	Writers' effects	Prepositions	Article	Dialogue News report Informative letter Speech	Prefixes Defining and non-defining relative causes Past tenses	Sentence punctuation: Semi-colons Commas
Unit 8: Aiming high	Writers' effects	Spelling Homophones	Article Internet news article	News report Journal entry	Parts of speech Linking words	
Unit 9: In deep water	Writers' effects Inference	Speech	Article Novel	Encyclopedia entry Journal entry		Punctuation: Apostrophes Semi-colons Commas
Unit 10: Losing sleep	Writers' effects	Prepositions Synonyms Raise / rise / arise	Article Short story	Informative leaflet Formal report	Complex sentences Conditional sentences	Commas
Unit 11: Sub-zero	Writers' effects	Paraphrase Sentence structure Synonyms	Article Journal entry	Advertisement Letter/email Magazine article	Complex sentences	
Unit 12: Seeing double	Writers' effects Identifying facts	Sentence structure Synonyms Spelling	Report Newspaper article	Summary Transcript of an interview Letter	Prefixes	

Unit 1: Rocket science

A Reading

1   Read the letter below.

Passage A: New Year's Eve fireworks

Dear Mum and Dad

Happy New Year! Hope you had a good New Year's Eve. I had the most amazing time here in Dubai, watching the biggest firework display ever – an **extravaganza** lasting six minutes, which set a new world record for a single **coordinated** display. The 500 000 fireworks were set off from 400 firing locations, **synchronised** by 100 computers. It took the **technicians** ten months to plan!

There was a countdown to midnight in fireworks in both roman and arabic numerals. Organisers said they wanted to create a burst of light to imitate a sunrise and dazzle spectators with a United Arab Emirates flag that could also break records for being the largest ever made of fireworks. They certainly did that!

I was down with thousands of watchers standing by the fountains at Burj Khalifa, the world's tallest tower, which was used as a backdrop for the display. Everyone got there early and the anticipation beforehand was **electric**; it wasn't only the children who were excited! The Burj is shaped like a rocket itself, and was the launch pad for thousands of smaller rockets. It was turned into a whole series of famous monuments, like the Eiffel Tower, by patterns of light flashing on it. And that was just a small part of it...

... it was a helter-skelter, with showers of sparks sliding down it. It was an **incandescent** pine tree with thousands of starry branches. It was a castle unleashing arrows of fire. Down below there was an orchard of trees bursting into blossom; there were pulsing globes like dandelion heads sending out seeds; there were tiered birthday cakes with exploding candles. **Iridescent** rings climbed the tower. **Scintillating** fountains leapt up to meet the cascades of light. Bouquets of bright flowers of every hue filled the sky.

Everyone was holding up their phone to capture the images, holding their breath, **mesmerised**. It was too much to take in; there were too many places to look **simultaneously**. The soundtrack of sci-fi film-type music matched the display of dancing light and water, and made it a space-age experience. There was huge applause at the end, cheering and whistling that went on for ages. It was unforgettable, and I really wish you could have seen it too.

Maybe next year! I'm really enjoying the job and the lifestyle, so I'll still be here then!

Love,

Lee

B Language and style

2 Give meanings for the following words, as they are used in Passage A. Look up any words you do not know, but first try to guess from the **prefix** or stem of the word. The first one has been done for you as an example.

a extravaganza *spectacle* _____

b coordinated _____

c synchronised _____

d technicians _____

e electric _____

f incandescent _____

g iridescent _____

h scintillating _____

i mesmerised _____

j simultaneously _____

3 **a** Next to each of the above words, write which part of speech it is, as used in the passage.
   b Study the words and then write out without looking (in a notebook) those you did not know how to spell.

C Comprehension and summary

4 Re-read the fourth paragraph of Passage A and comment on:
   a the sentence structure and its effect

   _____

   _____

   _____

   _____

   _____

   _____

   b the vocabulary and its effect

   _____

   _____

   _____

   _____

   _____

5 Select relevant material from the passage and write a news report in six paragraphs, with a suitable headline, for the next day's local newspaper.

_____

_____

_____

_____

_____

_____

_____

_____

_____

_____

_____

_____

_____

_____

_____

_____

_____

_____

_____

_____

_____

_____

_____

_____

_____

_____

_____

_____

_____

_____

_____

D Reading

6   Read the following encyclopedia article.

Passage B: Facts about fireworks

Fireworks are believed to have been invented more than 2000 years ago in China, where they were used in the form of firecrackers to accompany many festivities, in order to ward off evil and invoke prosperity. It is believed that the first firecrackers were actually accidental: chunks of bamboo thrown onto a fire. (Bamboo traps air inside the segments so that when heated, it expands and bursts through the sides, and this could have started the idea.) China is the largest manufacturer and exporter of fireworks in the world; 90% of all fireworks originate from there. They are still made by hand, and it is a hazardous job assembling the sections of the cardboard tubes.

In 1240, the Arabs acquired knowledge of gunpowder, and in the same century firecrackers arrived in Europe, with the crusaders or Marco Polo. The key ingredient in making fireworks is gunpowder, which consists of saltpetre (potassium nitrate), charcoal and sulphur. Early fireworks were enjoyed less for the show than for the sound; simple gunpowder explodes quickly with a terrific bang but with <u>little</u> colour. Over time, people discovered that using chemical compounds with greater amounts of oxygen made the explosives burn brighter and longer. At first fireworks were only orange and white. In the Middle Ages, new colours were achieved by adding different minerals. They had <u>least</u> success with blue. This became available with the discovery of copper compounds, but this is an unstable metal and so is <u>less</u> frequently used.

It wasn't until the 1800s that fireworks developed into what we know today. Italy was the first country in Europe to truly master and experiment with pyrotechnics, by loading firecrackers into cannons and shooting them into the air. Multi-hued displays were an innovation of the 1830s, when metals that burn at high temperatures and create colours, sparks and noises were added to gunpowder. The Italians are still at the forefront of pyrotechnic development,

and the phenomenal New Year display in Dubai in 2014 was masterminded by the Italian-American Phil Grucci.

Every year, people in China celebrate the invention of the firecracker on 18th April. Fireworks are also an integral part of the Chinese New Year celebrations. The big occasion for fireworks in the UK is Guy Fawkes Night (5th November) to celebrate the failure of the Gunpowder Plot to blow up parliament. France uses fireworks to celebrate Bastille Day, commemorating the storming of the prison during the French Revolution. Firework displays are also a major part of Independence Day celebrations in the United States.

The world record for the largest firework display before January 2014 in Dubai consisted of 77 282 fireworks set off in Kuwait in November 2011 as part of the country's 50th anniversary celebrations. The largest firework rocket – 13 kilograms – was produced and launched in Portugal in 2010. The biggest annual firework display event in Europe is the International Festival concert held in Edinburgh, Scotland, in which no <u>fewer</u> than a million fireworks are set off in <u>less</u> than an hour. A string of firecrackers lasting 22 hours marked the New Year's Day celebrations in Hong Kong in 1996. The world's largest single firework was seen at a festival in Japan in 1988; the burst was over a kilometre across and the shell weighed over half a tonne. A rocket can reach speeds of 240 kilometres per hour, and the shell can reach as high as 200 metres. People will always see the explosion of a firework before hearing it. This is because although they both travel in waves, light travels at 1080 million kilometres per hour whereas sound travels only at 1225 kilometres per hour.

In public shows today, specialists use computers to control the electronic ignition of fireworks, as well as to synchronise the aerial bursts with music. Firework displays are becoming ever more spectacular and are an established way of celebrating any global, national or local event or anniversary.

4

E Language and style

7 **a** Underline the **passive verb** forms in Passage **B** e.g. *are believed*.

b Explain why passive rather than active verb forms are used in certain types of text.

_____

_____

_____

_____

8 Look at the five underlined words in Passage **B** and consider how they are used. Fill the blanks in the paragraph below with one of these words. (You may want to use some words more than once, and some not at all.)

few	fewer	fewest	a few	little	less	least	a little

There are _____ signs of fireworks losing popularity as a form of entertainment.

Gradually, private firework shows are becoming _____ common and are being

replaced by public events. This means that the injuries caused by fireworks are _____,

but they are still a cause of damage to property, unintended fires, maiming of children and

traumatising of animals. _____ people argue that fireworks are destructive in

many senses, and that the expense and waste of natural resources cannot be justified in return for

_____ moments of pleasure, but there is _____ public debate on the

subject, and unlikely to be, given that they have been around for so long.

9 Use *given that* (used in the last sentence of the paragraph above) correctly in a sentence of your own.

_____

_____

F Comprehension and summary

10 **a** In which century did fireworks become known in Europe?

_____

b Express in your own words what happened to fireworks in the 1830s.

_____

_____

_____

_____

c Which country held the world record for a coordinated firework display before New Year's
Eve 2014?

_____

d Explain in your own words why we see fireworks before we hear them.

_____

e Express the following phrases in your own words.

   i _invoke prosperity_

   _____

   ii _multi-hued displays were an innovation_

   _____

   iii _still at the forefront_

   _____

11 **In one sentence each, summarise what Passage B says about:**

a the Chinese and fireworks

_____

_____

_____

_____

b the Italians and fireworks

_____

_____

_____

_____

c how fireworks are made

_____

_____

_____

_____

12 **Write a one-paragraph summary of the history of fireworks.**

_____

_____

_____

_____

_____

_____

_____

G Directed writing

13   Write a blog article called 'Who needs fireworks?' Engage with some of the ideas and use some
     of the facts contained in Passages A and B in order to present the view that too much money is
     wasted on this form of brief, childish and destructive entertainment.

_____

_____

_____

_____

_____

_____

_____

_____

_____

_____

_____

_____

_____

_____

_____

_____

_____

_____

_____

_____

_____

_____

_____

_____

_____

_____

_____

_____

_____

_____

_____

_____

H Composition

Descriptive writing

a Describe the environment and atmosphere of a venue waiting for an exciting event to start.
Answer the following questions:

- Where is the venue and what kind of place is it?
- What is the event and what kind of crowd has gathered?
- How are the people showing their excitement while they are waiting?

b Give an account of a real or imaginary experience of witnessing a sensational show.
Include details about the following:

- What kind of show was it?
- When and where did you go to see it, and who did you go with?
- What were the highlights and memorable parts of the show?

Narrative writing

c Write a story which involves an explosion.
Include the following aspects:

- the scene and atmosphere where the event occurs
- the characters involved and their roles and relationships
- the events that lead up to the climax of the story.

d Continue this story opening: 'I had been really looking forward to New Year's Eve ...'
Think about how you can achieve the following:

- convey the personality and circumstances of the main character
- include some significant dialogue with at least one other character
- explain what happened to spoil their expectations and end with a reference to the opening.

Unit 2: Bear essentials

A Reading

1   Read the article below.

Passage A: How the teddy got its name

A few people, perhaps of the kind who like to **amass** curious snippets of information, could probably tell you that the children's cuddly toy known as a 'teddy bear' is so called after Theodore ('Teddy') Roosevelt, who was President of the United States from 1901 to 1909. Far fewer could tell you just why a US President should have given his name to an object which by 1907 was selling almost a million a year.

All accounts are agreed upon the fact that early in life Roosevelt suffered from asthma and that his father believed that fresh air and exercise would improve his health. As a result, the future President became keen on outdoor pursuits and even studied to be a naturalist before taking up politics. However, he still continued to hunt, a very fashionable sport at the time.

And so it was that in 1902, while the President was taking time off from solving a border **dispute** in Mississippi, that the incident took place which linked his name for ever with the little furry creature. Roosevelt had had a bad day and shot nothing at all, so the guides, not wishing the **expedition** to be a failure, sent out dogs to track down a bear for the President to shoot. Here, however, accounts differ: some say that the black bear which they cornered was old and exhausted; others that it was a lost bear cub which was tracked down. Whichever was the case, Roosevelt refused to shoot it, saying that he considered this would be **unsporting**.

A political cartoonist called Clifford K. Berryman heard the story and made a drawing of the incident for the *Washington Post* (and in a second version of the cartoon he reduced the size of the bear, which may have given rise to the idea that it was a cub). The cartoon was so popular that Berryman depicted the young bear in other drawings of Roosevelt. The President's name was now firmly linked with bears, but how did his nickname of 'Teddy' come to be given to the toy bear? The owner of a New York toy shop, Morris Mitchom, asked the President if he could call

the bears in his shop, which his wife made, 'Teddy's Bears', to which Roosevelt agreed. Mitchom then founded the Ideal Toy and Novelty Company, which was to become one of the biggest toy companies in the United States.

However, the Mitchoms were not the first to make toy bears. Richard Steiff, a member of a German family firm, invented a bear with jointed limbs in 1902. This he **exhibited** at the 1903 Leipzig Spring Fair. The creature was a metre high, fierce-looking and heavy, and had the effect of scaring off potential customers rather than attracting them – with the exception of an American importer, Borgfeldt, who thought he recognised a way of cashing in on the popularity of the bear in the Roosevelt story. He ordered 3000 of them: the teddy bear boom had begun. Early examples of the teddy bear are now worth a fortune: a 1904 Steiff bear was sold for $110000 in 1994.

Since then, generations of children – and adults – have been **entranced** by this domesticated version of one of nature's fiercest predators, now made of every possible material from wool and wood to modern **synthetics** such as nylon. The teddy has featured as the hero of immensely popular books such as *Winnie-the-Pooh*, *Rupert Bear*, *The Jungle Book* and the *Paddington Bear* series, and its image appears on keyrings, greetings cards, mugs, posters and charity logos. It is also used to draw attention to the problems of bears that today live in threatened habitats, perhaps the most fitting way of **commemorating** President Roosevelt's refusal – 100 years ago – to shoot a defenceless bear for 'sport'.

9

B Language and style

2   Make sentences of your own which show the meaning of the words in bold in Passage A. Use a dictionary if you are not sure, but first try to work out their meaning from their prefixes, their context and their similarity to other words you already know. The first one has been done for you as an example.

a   amass _The researchers worked hard to **amass** a great deal of data._

_____

b   dispute _____

_____

c   expedition _____

_____

d   unsporting _____

_____

e   exhibited _____

_____

f   entranced _____

_____

g   synthetics _____

_____

h   commemorating _____

_____

3   Circle all the pairs of dashes, brackets and commas in Passage A. As you can see, they form a parenthesis (i.e. a word or phrase of comment or explanation inserted into a sentence which is grammatically complete without it). Commas are the most subtle, and brackets the least, because of their relative visual impact.

Put a variety of parenthetical punctuation into the following sentences, considering how close you think the extra information is to the content of the main sentence. Some sentences may need more than one parenthesis.

a   Wild apes have no need of language and have not developed it but tame ones can use it as a tool for communicating with each other.

b   Each slaughtered ape is a loss to the local community a loss to humanity as a whole and is a hole torn in the ecology of our planet.

c   The skills of language and counting essential for negotiating trade can be taught to orang-utans who are less social primates than chimpanzees in a matter of weeks.

d   Fifteen million years a small gap in the broad scale of evolution is an immense period in terms of everyday life.

e   Gorilla mothers prefer to cradle their babies on their left sides a feature shared with humans and there have been cases of them showing maternal behaviour to human children.

C Comprehension and summary

4 Referring to Passage A, say whether the following statements are True (T), False (F) or Don't know (D), and give reasons.

a More people know who the bear is named after than know why.

_____

b Roosevelt was more of a hunter than a wildlife supporter.

_____

c The bear Roosevelt refused to shoot was a cub.

_____

d The Ideal Toy and Novelty Company was the first to manufacture teddy bears in the USA.

_____

e The customers at the Leipzig Spring Fair in 1903 found the bears very attractive.

_____

5 **a** Highlight the material in Passage **A** that you would use to explain how the teddy got its name. Write each point separately below, in your own words as far as possible, ordering them logically.

_____

_____

_____

_____

_____

_____

_____

_____

_____

_____

b Link the points to create no more than two sentences.

_____

_____

_____

_____

_____

_____

_____

D Reading

6   Read the short story below.

Passage B: A tale of a bear

There was once a lady who lived in an old manor house on the border of a big forest, high up in the North. This lady had a pet bear she was very fond of. It had been found in the forest half-dead of hunger, so small and helpless that it had to be brought up on the bottle by the lady and her old cook. This was several years ago and now it had grown up to be a big bear so strong that he could have slain a cow and carried it away if he had wanted to.

But he did not want to; he was a most amiable bear who did not dream of harming anybody, man or beast. He used to sit outside his kennel and look with his small, intelligent eyes most amicably at the cattle grazing in the field nearby. The children used to ride on his back and had more than once been found asleep in his kennel between his two paws. The three Lapland dogs loved to play all sorts of games with him, pull his ears and his stump of a tail and tease him in every way, but he did not mind in the least.

He had a fine appetite, but his friend the cook saw to it that he got his fill. Bears are vegetarians if they have a chance; fruit is what they like best. Bears look clumsy and slow in their movements, but try a bear with an apple tree and you will soon find out that he can easily beat any schoolchild at that activity.

There had been some difficulties about the bee-hives; he had been punished for this by being put on the chain for two days with a bleeding nose and he had never done it again. Otherwise he was only put on the chain at night (for a bear is apt to get somewhat ill-tempered if kept on a chain) or on Sundays when his mistress went to spend the afternoon with her married sister, who lived in a solitary house on the other side of the mountain lake, a good hour's walk through the dense forest. It was not considered good for him to wander about in the forest with all its temptations. Now he knew quite well what it meant when his mistress put him on the chain on Sundays, with a friendly tap on his head and the promise of an apple on her return if he had been good during her absence. He was sorry but resigned.

One Sunday when the lady had chained him up as usual and was about half-way through the forest, she suddenly thought she heard the cracking of a tree branch on the winding footpath behind her. She looked back and was horrified to see the bear coming along full-speed. In a minute he had joined her, panting and sniffing, to take up his usual place, dog-fashion, at her heels. The lady was very angry: she was already late for lunch, there was no time to take him back home, she did not want him to come with her, and besides, it was very naughty of him to have disobeyed her and broken away from his chain. She ordered him in her severest voice to go back at once, menacing him with her umbrella. He stopped a moment and looked at her with his cunning eyes, but then kept on sniffing at her. When the lady saw that he had even lost his new collar, she got still more angry and hit him on the nose with her umbrella so hard that it broke in two. He stopped again, shook his head, and opened his big mouth several times as if he wanted to say something. Then he turned round and began to shuffle back the way he had come, stopping now and then to look at the lady till at last she lost sight of him.

When the lady came home in the evening, he was sitting in his usual place outside his kennel looking very sorry for himself. The lady was still very angry with him and she told him that he would have no apple and no supper, and that he would be chained for two days as an extra punishment.

The old cook, who loved the bear as if he had been her son, rushed out from the kitchen. 'What are you scolding him for, missus?' she asked. 'He has been as good as gold the whole day, bless him! He has been sitting here looking the whole time towards the gate for you to come back.'

It had been a different bear!

From *The Story of San Michele*, Axel Munthe Estate and
Hodder & Stoughton Ltd. (John Murray Press)

E Language and style

7   Write sentences about the bear in Passage B using ideas expressed in the following grammatical structures.

   a   Not only … but also

   _____

   _____

b Never before ...

_____

_____

c Neither ... nor

_____

_____

d No longer ...

_____

_____

e Not so much as a ...

_____

_____

8 **a** Explain how the writer achieves the effect of surprise in Passage **B**.

_____

_____

_____

_____

_____

_____

_____

_____

b Explain how the writer evokes sympathy for the bear in Passage **B**.

_____

_____

_____

_____

_____

_____

_____

_____

F Comprehension and summary

9 **a** Summarise the story of Passage **B** in one paragraph.

_____

_____

_____

_____

_____

_____

_____

_____

b Give the reasons, in sentences, why humans find bears attractive, using ideas stated in or inferred from Passages **A** and **B**.

_____

_____

_____

_____

_____

_____

_____

_____

_____

G Directed writing

10 Read the information in the fact box below.

Great apes survival project

FACT

Population: over past 20 years, surveys indicate substantial and continual decline from 100 000 individuals reported in 1980

Habitat: Cameroon and Congo basin and other central African equatorial regions; once virgin rainforest

Characteristics: share 99% of human DNA; live for 60 years; capable of intelligent communication with the comprehension level of a six-year-old child; can learn sign language; have IQ of 80, similar to many humans

Threats: hunters earn $35 for a dead male silverback gorilla; orphaned babies cannot survive; could be extinct in 5–10 years because of destruction of habitat and slaughter for cheap bush meat with snares and guns; commercial mining for coltan, used in mobile phones, games consoles and military aircraft, has already made some gorilla populations extinct

Aims: appoint rangers ('ecoguards') and provide vehicles and communication equipment to monitor and protect animals; construct wildlife corridors to link fragmented habitats; educate locals on value of apes for eco-tourism; gain legal rights to protect apes and chimpanzees and their right to life and liberty, and freedom from torture and medical experimentation, because of their similarity to humans.

11 Write an informative article for your school magazine to explain the project.

_____

_____

_____

_____

_____

_____

_____

_____

_____

_____

_____

_____

_____

_____

_____

_____

_____

_____

_____

_____

_____

_____

_____

_____

_____

_____

_____

_____

_____

_____

_____

_____

_____

_____

12   **Read the following fact box about spectacled bears.**

The spectacled bear campaign

FACT

Population: approx. 3000 left; population has collapsed because of destruction of rainforest during last 30 years

Habitat: around the Andes in South America, in cloud forests and Andean moorland; found in countries such as Venezuela, Argentina and Peru

Characteristics: only bear in this continent; also known as the Andean bear; has bands of colour around the eyes; shaggy fur; very shy; smaller than other bears; nocturnal; solitary; excellent climber; eats mainly fruit and nuts; sometimes carnivore; cubs born November–February in rainy season

Threats: bears frequently killed for sport or by farmers protecting crops; cubs sometimes captured and kept in appalling conditions for the amusement of their captors; discovered only in second half of 20th century; may disappear before end of the 21st century

Aims: to rescue bears from captivity in small cages and remove them to specially created sanctuaries

Other information: one of the causes adopted by the Rainforest Alliance

13 Write a speech persuading students at your school to help raise funds for the spectacled bears.

H Composition

Descriptive writing

a 'The Circus'. Write a descriptive composition with this title.
Include details about the following:

- the sounds, smells and sights around and in the tent
- the spectacles to be seen in the ring
- the feelings and responses of the audience.

b Describe your surroundings on a safari expedition, and give your thoughts and feelings about being in this setting.

Think about how to include sufficient specific detail about the following to make them seem real:

- weather and temperature
- landscape, vegetation, wildlife
- companions, vehicle, clothing and equipment.

Narrative writing

c Write a story set in a forest or jungle.

Think about the following:

- what part will be played by the setting?
- who are the characters and why are they there?
- will the outcome be happy or sad?

d 'But it was a case of mistaken identity'. Write a story that ends with this sentence.

Decide on the following:

- what is going to be mistaken for what
- how the misunderstanding comes about
- how the truth is revealed at the end.

Unit 3: Simply flying

A Reading

1 **Read the article below.**

Passage A: My life at TopFlight

It's 8:00 a.m. Monday morning, and Manchester Airport is closed due to fog. As a result, three TopFlight flights are unable to land at the airport. In the terminal, over 300 TopFlight passengers are becoming increasingly anxious – many have appointments to keep. We are then advised that Air Traffic Control has diverted the incoming aircraft to Leeds airport. So … three aircraft in Leeds and their corresponding passengers in Manchester. And my job? To sort it out!

Obviously this kind of **scenario** is unusual – but it can happen. As airport manager for northern England, I am responsible for overseeing all the TopFlight ground operations at both Manchester and Leeds airports. Essentially, this means that I look after all TopFlight activities at the airport, up until the point the aircraft takes off. This includes all aspects of passenger services (check-in, sales desks, departures and arrivals), as well as the behind-the-scenes operations such as baggage handling.

My time is divided between both airports, but as there are far more TopFlight flights to and from Manchester than Leeds (23 per day compared to five), the larger proportion of my time is spent at Manchester.

At both airports, we work in close partnership with our handling agents, and a crucial part of my role is overseeing their practice to ensure that TopFlight passengers receive the very best service as they proceed through the airport and on to their flight. I organise regular training sessions and group activities with all our service staff.

Much of my job is about building strong relationships and partnerships, and I liaise closely with other airport managers to ensure that the interests of TopFlight are properly represented. TopFlight already has an established presence at Manchester (we are the third-largest airline there), but it lies with me to see that our profile remains high with the authorities, so that TopFlight continues to receive a good service.

Obviously, safety is top of the agenda, and I am responsible for ensuring that we comply with all the standards and regulations set down by the relevant government bodies.

As a scheduled airline operating high-frequency, short-haul flights, another critical measure of our performance is the punctuality of our flights. As so many factors within the airport environment can affect punctuality, I continually **monitor** every aspect of our operation at both airports so that I can quickly identify areas of weakness and put measures in place to **rectify** these. Airports are complex environments and so, for everything to run smoothly, it's very important that everyone works as a team. Excellent communication skills are therefore essential. At times it can also be a stressful place, and so the ability to remain calm and maintain a sense of humour is also crucial! One of the things I really enjoy about my job is interacting with a wide variety of people – from passengers to airport senior management.

I keep fully up to date with what's going on at the airline by travelling down to the TopFlight offices at London Stansted airport regularly to meet with colleagues – including my **counterparts** from other TopFlight airports. We all share ideas and experiences so that we can continually improve the way in which we work. It's also my opportunity to give **feedback** about what's happening at my airports.

To succeed in this role, you need to be adaptable and flexible, as no two days are ever the same and you have to deal with everything. It's not a job for people who like to **meticulously** plan out every minute of their day! But I really enjoy the pace and variety – and I can honestly say it's never boring.

20

B Language and style

2 The underlined words in Passage **A** have more than one meaning. Choose the one which is being used in this context.

a	corresponding:	letter-writing	matching	respective
b	essentially:	necessarily	mainly	basically
c	proportion:	size	ratio	part
d	critical:	vital	finding fault	in a crisis
e	deal:	trade	sort out	distribute

3 The following words from Passage **A** are useful but tricky to spell. Look at the bold 'hot-spot' (difficult part) in each word for a few seconds, then cover the word and try to write it correctly from memory.

Think of a rule or mnemonic (way of remembering) to help you remember the spelling of those words you find difficult.

a cru**ci**al _____   **f** enviro**nm**ent _____

b re**cei**ve _____   **g** ex**cell**ent _____

c l**iai**se _____   **h** coll**eague**s _____

d s**ch**eduled _____   **i** su**ccee**d _____

e pu**nct**uality _____   **j** **oppor**tunity _____

4 Give synonyms for these words, which are in bold in Passage **A**:

a scenario _situation_   **d** counterparts _____

b monitor _____   **e** feedback _____

c rectify _____   **f** meticulously _____

5 Put as many prefixes as possible on to the following stems.
For example: -prove   improve, approve, reprove, disprove

a -vert _____

b -port _____

c -sult _____

d -sent _____

e -ply _____

6 Write a sentence containing each word below to show the difference in meaning between the words in each pair. The first one has been done for you as an example.

a proceed _When the alarm goes off, please proceed to the nearest exit._

precede _A brief presentation will precede the debate._

b lie _____

lay _____

21

   c affect _____

       effect _____

   d continuous _____

       continual _____

   e principal _____

       principle _____

   f whose _____

       who's _____

   g uninterested _____

       disinterested _____

7 **Circle the single dashes and hyphens used in the text. First work out the rules for their usage and then give other examples of your own.**

   a Dashes have a space either side and are used singly to: _____

       _____

       For example: _____

       _____

   b Hyphens, which do not have spaces before or after, are used to: _____

       _____

       For example: _____

       _____

8 **a** Who do you think is the audience for Passage **A**?

       _____

       _____

       _____

   b List the features of the passage that are typical of spoken informal language.

       _____

       _____

       _____

       _____

       _____

       _____

       _____

C Comprehension and summary

9 In a paragraph, give the facts about the airline in Passage **A**.

_____

_____

_____

_____

_____

_____

_____

_____

_____

_____

10 In a paragraph, describe the qualities needed for the job of airport manager.

_____

_____

_____

_____

_____

_____

_____

_____

_____

11 In a paragraph, summarise the responsibilities and tasks of an airport manager.

_____

_____

_____

_____

_____

_____

_____

_____

_____

D Reading

12   Read the article below.

Passage B: Junior jet set

An estimated 7 million children a year travel alone by air, many as young as seven. Some are travelling between home and their boarding schools in the UK, particularly from Asia. Last year, one airline alone carried 3000 flyers aged between five and 11. Specialist staff are provided by airlines, known in the trade as 'aunties', to escort these transcontinental commuters from check-in to aircraft. They have to reassure nervous flyers and give them cuddles, and even clean clothes if necessary.

The children tend to be treated as VIPs, being seated and fed before the other passengers. They pass the time with video games and puzzles, and are so well looked after that many say they prefer flying solo to travelling with their families!

At the other end, the 'unmins' or 'ums' as they are nicknamed (standing for 'unaccompanied minors') are collected from the plane and delivered to the designated adult meeting the child.

Some US airlines charge for this service, but most European and Asian ones do not. Teenagers up to 16 or 17 – depending on the airline – are called 'young passengers' and are still accompanied to the pick-up.

Things rarely go wrong, but it has been known for a child to be flown to the wrong destination, and cancelled connecting flights can create the headache of having to put up the stranded youngster in a hotel.

E Comprehension and summary

13 Read the tips below.

> ## Tips for the parents of 'unmins'
>
> **a** Train your child to recite their name, address and phone number.
> **b** Give your child some money.
> **c** Take novice flyers on a tour of the airport before the day they fly.
> **d** Arrange for them to travel at off-peak times.
> **e** Avoid night flights.
> **f** Don't leave the airport until you have seen the plane take off.
> **g** Book an aisle seat.
> **h** Ask for your child to be seated near other children.

14 Infer the reason for each tip in the box in question E13. The first one has been done for you as an example.

a *So that if they get separated from their 'auntie', they can explain who they are and their parents can be contacted.*

b _____

c _____

d _____

e _____

f _____

g _____

h _____

15 Using information and ideas from Passages **A** and **B**, write an interview with a child flyer by the airport manager, who has been called by an 'auntie' to find out about a problem the child is having.

AM: Hello. My name is Sue Watson and I'm the airport manager here. What can I do to help?

Child: _____

_____

_____

_____

_____

_____

_____

_____

25

F Directed writing

16   Read the recruitment advertisement below.

Want to work for us?

Looking for a new challenge with an interesting and dynamic company?
Take a look at these exciting career opportunities at TopFlight ...

Come fly with us...

We are currently recruiting cabin crew for our base at London Stansted.

Our cabin crew must ensure that our customers' safety and comfort come first and that they create a memorable experience by providing friendly and courteous service at all times. The job is busy and can be physically demanding. Cabin crew have to be prepared to work on any day of the year, any time of the day.

You must be:

- friendly and approachable
- mature in attitude and behaviour
- able to remain calm and efficient under pressure
- an excellent communicator with people of all ages and cultures
- a team player
- flexible and adaptable
- able to take the initiative
- willing to accept guidance.

Minimum requirements:

- age 20+
- height 1.58 m to 1.82 m with weight in proportion to height
- physically fit and able to pass a medical assessment
- fluent in English, both spoken and written
- good standard in at least one other language
- able to swim 25 m
- possess a passport allowing unrestricted travel within Europe.

If you meet all of our person specifications and minimum requirements, please request an application form from:

Cabin Crew Applications
TopFlight Airline Company Ltd
London Stansted Airport
Essex, UK

27

17   Write a job application letter to the personnel manager of TopFlight, saying why the job would suit you and why you would suit the job. You may also add any extra material of your own that you consider relevant.

_____

_____

_____

_____

_____

_____

_____

_____

_____

_____

_____

_____

_____

_____

_____

_____

_____

_____

_____

_____

_____

_____

_____

_____

_____

_____

G Composition

Descriptive writing

a Describe the atmosphere of a busy airport, referring to particular people and situations that you observe.

To create atmosphere, you need to refer to the following:

- what can be seen and its effect
- what can be heard and its effect
- how it makes the observer feel.

b Describe, in role, an hour in the day of a flight attendant, including your thoughts and feelings during that time.

Answer the following questions:

- What tense will you use?
- Where you will be during that hour?
- Will you write an account of a typical hour or describe an atypical event?

Narrative writing

c Write a story that involves a farewell scene.

- Who are the characters?
- When, where and why are they saying goodbye?
- How can the ending be made unpredictable or ironic?

d 'An unforgettable plane journey'. Write a story with this title.

- In what way was it unforgettable?
- At what point in the journey will the narrative start?
- What will the last sentence be?

Unit 4: On the ball

A Reading

1   Read the article below.

Passage A: Love it or hate it

In viewing terms, the World Cup is twice as big as any other sporting event on the planet. But just because it's big doesn't mean it's beautiful; football can bring out the worst in people: it can make them obsessive and boring; it can make them prejudiced and intolerant; it can make them violent and destructive. But despite the corruption and cynicism surrounding it, football has never lost its appeal.

Football weaves itself into whichever culture embraces it, appealing to people who have nothing else in common but who each have a personal passion for the game and are addicted to its spontaneity. Packaged into 90 minutes are heroes and villains, hope and despair, skill and drama: a miniature war with flags and armies.

Football has an astonishing ability to cross borders and barriers, as between German and British troops in no-man's-land in World War I. It seems so natural to share the kicking of a ball, and the basic structure of the game is amazingly simple: two opposing sides attempt to push a spherical object into the other's goal. Played informally, football has great flexibility, with no set number of players, no particular type of pitch and no essential equipment except something to kick and something to define the goal mouth.

Anthropologists have explained people's universal and enduring fascination with football as being a replacement and compensation for the hunter-gatherer instincts which have no outlet in the 21st century. It is a substitute for the quest, combining the necessary elements of a group of people, adrenalin and the prospect of reward – the holy grail of winning the cup. Many ancient civilisations – China, Japan, Greece and Rome – all had equivalents of the game, which they exported, as did the British, to parts of their far-flung empires.

Documentary evidence dates football back to 1175 in England, when Shrove Tuesday, immediately before the beginning of Lent and abstinence, was the big day in the footballing calendar. During the 1830s, matches were becoming nothing better than a series of punch-ups, so they were stamped out

briefly. By 1863, the Football Association had been set up in London between 11 clubs after a meeting at Cambridge University to agree a set of rules. The people who attended the meeting were physical education teachers from famous public schools and 'old boys' who had continued to play the game after leaving school. By the 1870s, the game had become professional, and international fixtures were being arranged with countries in South America and northern Europe. This is the origin of the modern World Cup, following the evolution of FIFA as an international football organisation, and live radio coverage, which became possible in 1927.

No other single sport has brought together nations and individuals so much or provided more pleasure over a longer period of time. Football has also, however, given the world things it would be much better without: riots, vandalism, hooliganism and tribalism. More recently, it's become a vehicle for an upsurge in nationalism, racism and fascism, the full consequences of which are still fearfully awaited. It's been taken over by the mass media; huge sums of money are involved in advertising, sponsorship, transfer fees, merchandise and broadcasting rights. It's turned into soap opera, with players (and their families) treated as idols and celebrities – rather than mere mortals with skilful feet – and deprived of a private life by the feeding-frenzied tabloid sharks.

B Language and style

2 **a** Circle the **apostrophes** (') in Passage **A**. Explain the two usages of apostrophes.

We use apostrophes either when we _____

(for example: _____)

or when we _____

(for example: _____).

An apostrophe after the final s of a word, unless it is a name, indicates that _____

_____

(for example: _____).

b In the passage there are examples of *it's* with an apostrophe and *its* without an apostrophe. What is the difference?

We use an apostrophe in *it's* if _____

_____

whereas *its* without an apostrophe is used to _____

_____

3 Circle the **semi-colons** (;) in Passage **A** and define their usage by filling the gaps below.

Semi-colons, which are used sparingly and only for a good reason, have the same function as

_____; they are used when the preceding sentence has a _____

with the following sentence. They can also be used to separate _____.

4 Underline the 'hot-spots' in the following words from Passage A. Look up the meaning of any words you are not sure of. Cover them up, then practise writing them correctly.

a fascination _____

b beautiful _____

c vehicle _____

d attempt _____

e cynicism _____

f professional _____

g prejudiced _____

h equivalent _____

i spontaneity _____

j skilful _____

k miniature _____

l calendar _____

C Comprehension and summary

5 Change the following words from Passage A to their active verb form (e.g. hatred – hate).

  a beautiful _____

  b destructive _____

  c enduring _____

  d abstinence _____

  e pleasure _____

  f celebrities _____

6 Give synonymous words or phrases for the following compound words used in Passage A.

  a hunter-gatherer _____

  b far-flung _____

  c no-man's-land _____

  d punch-ups _____

  e feeding-frenzied _____

7 Highlight the relevant points in Passage A and write a summary of the history of football, using your own words as far as possible.

_____

_____

_____

_____

_____

_____

_____

_____

_____

_____

_____

_____

_____

_____

_____

D Directed writing

8   Write a letter to the author of Passage **A**, responding to their opinions about football
     and giving your own views on the subject.

_____

_____

_____

_____

_____

_____

_____

_____

_____

_____

_____

_____

_____

_____

_____

_____

_____

_____

_____

_____

_____

_____

_____

_____

_____

_____

_____

_____

E Reading

9   **Read the article below.**

Passage B: Really royal

There has been a recent rise in interest in the game of real tennis, the ancestor of modern tennis and also the forerunner of squash, rackets and badminton. Although it is still a niche sport that has only 10 000 players in four countries – France, Britain, Australia and the USA – it is now on the up for the first time since the World War I started in 1914.

'Real' is a corruption of the word 'royal', and real tennis goes back to the shape of the court and the rules of tennis in medieval times, when it was a game played by kings, notably the French and English monarchs. When it was brought to England from France in the 1530s, Henry VIII was a keen player, despite his not inconsiderable bulk.

Modern lawn tennis is played outdoors on symmetrical and parallel-lined grass or clay courts, using fluorescent yellow balls and graphite racquets – although until comparatively recently the balls were white and the racquets were wooden and heavy. In the Middle Ages, tennis was an indoor game and the courts were not only huge – the size of banqueting halls – but also asymmetrical. Real tennis is a cross between tennis and squash; it is still played on an indoor court, one which has high black walls and a buttress or 'tambour', that is a sloping roof – but only on one side – against which every serve must bounce.

The spectators watch from a viewing gallery or 'penthouse'. The other end of the court is open and is referred to as the 'dedans'. The balls are solid, and therefore heavy. Even stranger, every court is different in size, although they all have the same markings. These are important because they enable the return of the ball even when normal rules of tennis are broken, such as the ball bouncing more than once. This makes the game less demanding in some ways than modern tennis, and attractive to older and less fit players – as well as total beginners – because they can still win points without having to run around too much.

An Australian club coach has this to say about this increasingly popular game, which now even makes it into the sports news from time to time: 'The rules and scoring system admittedly seem bizarre at first and take a bit of getting used to, but the fun of it is that it's a uniquely three-dimensional game. The ball comes at you from all angles, and there are lots of different options of how to play it. You have to become proficient at various types of shot, but mostly it's a question of learning how to read the game and use tactical skills, just like in chess. Most real tennis clubs are encouraging to potential players who phone up and say "I've heard or read about this game called real tennis. Can you tell me more about it? I'd love to give it a go!"'

F Language and style

10   **Draw lines to match the following words from Passage B to their meanings in the second column.**

a niche	strategic
b corruption	specialised
c asymmetrical	accomplished
d proficient	debasement
e tactical	lopsided

11 Look at the way direct speech is punctuated in Passage B. Fill in the gaps below to remind yourself of the rules for punctuating speech. The first one has been done for you as an example.

Within speech, most of the same punctuation rules apply as for normal writing, so that there needs to be a _full stop_ at the end of a sentence, provided that there is no continuation of the sentence after the end of the speech. If there is, then in place of the full stop we use a _____ or, if appropriate, a question mark or exclamation mark can be used. Even after a question or exclamation mark, the next word begins with a _____ letter rather than a _____ if it is continuing the sentence. If a sentence in speech is interrupted and then continued, there is a _____ before the break and again before the re-opening of the inverted commas. The continuation will begin with a small letter and not a capital because the _____ is also continuing. There must always be a punctuation mark of some kind before the closing _____. If a speech contains speech or quotation, then the inner speech must use the opposite kind of _____ from the outer speech, whether single or double.

12 Look at the following words from Passage **B** and formulate a spelling rule for double letters. Give other similar examples.

gallery   different   attractive   tennis   admittedly

Rule: _____

_____

_____

_____

Examples: _____

_____

_____

13 Look at the following words from Passage **B**. Work out the meanings of the prefixes, then use them to make other words.

fore(runner)   medi(eval)   sym(metrical)   para(llel)   en(couraging)

Meanings: _____

_____

_____

_____

Other words: _____

_____

_____

14   Passage B contains some idiomatic expressions. Use the following phrases in sentences of your own to show their meaning.

   a   on the up _____

   _____

   b   not inconsiderable _____

   _____

   c   a cross between _____

   _____

   d   from time to time _____

   _____

   e   give it a go _____

   _____

15   The following words from Passage **B** are difficult to spell. Use the Look, Cover, Write, Check method to learn them, then write them again three times each.

   ancestor _____

   fluorescent _____

   racquet _____

   bizarre _____

   uniquely _____

G Comprehension and summary

16   Using information from Passage B, write two paragraphs of not more than 75 words each about real tennis: a) the historical background of the game; b) the unusual features of the game.

   a   _____

   _____

   _____

   _____

   _____

   _____

   _____

   _____

   _____

   _____

   _____

b _____

_____

_____

_____

_____

_____

_____

_____

_____

_____

H Directed writing

17 Imagine you are a club coach answering a phone call from someone interested in taking up 'real' tennis. Write a sequence of five questions and answers to use as much as possible of the relevant material in Passage **B**.

Caller: I've heard about this game called real tennis. Can you tell me something about it?

Coach: _____

_____

_____

_____

_____

_____

_____

_____

_____

_____

_____

_____

_____

_____

_____

_____

_____

_____

_____

_____

_____

_____

_____

_____

_____

_____

_____

_____

_____

_____

_____

_____

I Composition

Descriptive writing

a Describe the experience of being in a large, noisy and uncontrolled crowd leaving a match.
- What has caused whatever mood the crowd is in?
- How are you feeling physically and emotionally?
- What are you afraid might happen?

b Describe the climactic minutes in a competition between two players.
- Set the scene and atmosphere, and describe the spectators.
- Describe the competitors and the point they have reached in the match.
- Focus on the final moves which determine the winner.

Narrative writing

c Write a story involving a small group of sports fans.
- Decide on your characters and how you will differentiate them.
- Begin with a dialogue planning something.
- Decide on the difficulties that will emerge and how they will be resolved.

d Write a story entitled 'The Turning Point' .
- What is the situation–event and who are the characters involved?
- What were the initial expectations and progress so far?
- What caused a sudden change, and what was the outcome?

Unit 5: Great rivers

A Reading

1   Read the article below.

Passage A: Amazon facts

What makes the Amazon the greatest river in the world is the volume of water that it carries; it **produces** 20% of the world's river water. Although the Nile river in Africa is the longest river in the world (at 6 650 kilometres long to the Amazon's approximate 6 280 kilometres), the Nile does not carry a 60th of the amount of water that the Amazon does, because the latter river drains the entire northern half of the South American continent. The torrential tropical rains deluge the rainforests with over 10 metres a year, and rainfall in the region is a near daily **occurrence**. The Amazon is also the world's widest river (6–10 kilometres), and the mouth of the Amazon, where it meets the sea, is so **deep** as well as wide that ocean-going ships have navigated its waters far inland. It becomes even wider when it floods in the wet season.

The precise source of the Amazon was only recently discovered, although the **origins** of most of the Earth's great rivers have been known for some time, and the quest to find the Amazon's origin in the most inaccessible part of the world had intrigued **explorers** for centuries. Determining the source of the Amazon has been so difficult because of a combination of unfriendly terrain, high altitudes, cold winds and the large number of potential headwater streams that needed to be investigated. What defines a river's origin is the most distant point from the mouth (as **measured** along the river's course and not by the way the crow flies) from which water flows year round along the main trunk of the river, not including the tributaries.

In 2001, a 22-member international team of mappers and explorers, **sponsored** by the National Geographic Society, claimed to have pin-pointed the source of the Amazon river. The team explored five different headwater streams in the Andes before they were **convinced** that they had **definitely** discovered the place where drops of water first collect to form the mighty Amazon. According to the team, the Amazon's origin is a small mountain stream that flows from the sides of Nevado Mismi, a 5 600-metre mountain in southern Peru. A global positioning system (GPS), linked to a network of satellites, was employed to precisely locate the source, which is less than 160 kilometres from the Pacific Ocean

Famously, the Amazon river is home to many exotic and **extreme** tropical creatures, such as catfish, anaconda (biggest snake) and piranha (most ferocious fish), as well as the macaws and tapirs that add their colours and sounds to the jungle.

B Language and style

2 Fill in the table below with the missing part(s) of speech that go with the word given (e.g. a suitable noun for 'produces' is 'product'). Each word is one of the words in bold in Passage A. In some cases you may be able to find more than one word that fits the part of speech, and in others none.

Noun	Adjective	Verb	Adverb
		produces	
occurrence			
	deep		
origins			
explorers			
		measured	
		sponsored	
		convinced	
			definitely
	extreme		

3 Circle all the commas in Passage A and study how they are used. Work out and define the five ways in which commas are used, giving an example of each.

a _____

_____

For example: _____

b _____

_____

For example: _____

c _____

_____

For example: _____

d _____

_____

For example: _____

e _____

_____

For example: _____

4 **a** Complex sentences are constructed by linking subordinate clauses to a main clause using connectives, and by adding participle phrases (present or past, with or without a preposition). Underline examples of different types of linking in Passage **A.**

b Link the three simple sentences below into **one complex sentence** in as many ways as you can. You may need to make changes to the grammar or word order. (Note that *and, but, so* and *or* form **compound** and not complex sentences.)

i The source of the Amazon has only recently been discovered.

ii The source is located 160 kilometres from the Pacific Ocean.

iii Explorers tried for centuries to discover the river's source.

_____

_____

_____

_____

_____

_____

_____

_____

_____

_____

_____

_____

_____

_____

_____

_____

_____

C Comprehension and summary

5 In two sentences, using connectives and participles, summarise the information in the first paragraph of Passage **A.**

_____

_____

_____

_____

_____

_____

D Reading

6 **Read the article below.**

Passage B: Life and death on the Nile

For Egyptians, farmers and fishermen, the Nile is not just a beautiful view, it is a gift, without which there could be no Egypt, only a scorched wasteland. In a country that does not receive much rainfall, the river is their livelihood. It covers only 4% of the country but its banks are where almost all of the 67 million Egyptians live. The Nile irrigates corn crops and citrus orchards, and provides water for herds of cows and for doing the laundry. Its seasons are the rhythms of the Egyptian way of life; when it floods every July, locals move to higher ground until it subsides three months later.

The waters of the Nile flow for nearly 7 000 kilometres, from the jungles of Uganda through the deserts of Sudan to arrive at Cairo, Africa's largest city. For centuries no one knew where it began, and the whereabouts of its source was a legend and a quest – a dangerous one, as the Nile contains crocodiles and intruders into the heart of Africa were often not welcomed by the native population. The source was finally discovered in the mid-19th century.

The world's longest river is a personality in myth as well as in reality. It features in many memorable scenes in the Bible and in literature, ancient and modern. It was assigned to the god Isis, to be honoured with offerings of food, and it was believed that the pharaohs could control it through their magical powers. The pyramids could not have been built without the means of transport provided by the great river.

Local stories tell of mythical creatures, some half-human and half-fish, which inhabit the river and sometimes take a fancy to humans and take them to live at the bottom; and of others which own the river and must be fed and kept happy or they will cause harm. The Egyptian queen Cleopatra was nicknamed the Serpent of Old Nile, and it was believed that the river mud had creative powers and produced snakes. Many films and books have used the romantic and threatening setting of the river, including the famous Agatha Christie detective novel *Death on the Nile*.

Since the advent of cruise liners and the influx of tourists, however, life on the riverbank has changed, and Egyptians say that the Nile is no longer theirs. Although it is, in fact, chemical fertilisers that are largely responsible, local opinion is that the leisure boats have polluted the water. They watch as the great city of Cairo continues to spread its garish hotels and grey apartment blocks along the banks in a ribbon development that shows no signs of stopping.

E Language and style

7 Read the extract below from Joseph Conrad's *Heart of Darkness*.

Passage C

Going up that river was like travelling back to the earliest beginnings of the world, when vegetation rioted on the earth and the big trees were kings. An empty stream, a great silence, an impenetrable forest. The air was warm, thick, heavy, sluggish. There was no joy in the brilliance of sunshine. The long stretches of the waterway ran on, deserted, into the gloom of overshadowed distances. On silvery sandbanks hippos and alligators sunned themselves side by side. The broadening waters flowed through a mob of wooded islands; you lost your way on that river as you would in a desert, and butted all day long against shoals, trying to find the channel, till you thought yourself bewitched and cut off for ever from everything you had known once – somewhere – far away – in another existence perhaps. There were moments when one's past came back to one, as it will sometimes when you have not a moment to spare to yourself; but it came in the shape of an unrestful and noisy dream, remembered with wonder amongst the overwhelming realities of this strange world of plants, and water, and silence. And this stillness of life did not in the least resemble a peace. It was the stillness of an implacable force brooding over an inscrutable intention. It looked at you with a vengeful aspect.

8 The extract describes the River Congo. Choose five words or phrases that convey the feeling of:

a mystery _____

_____

b threat _____

_____

9 In what ways does the description of the river in Passage **C** differ from the descriptions of the rivers in Passages **A** and **B**? Look at the difference in vocabulary and its effects.

_____

_____

_____

_____

_____

_____

_____

_____

_____

_____

_____

43

F Comprehension and summary

10 List the facts and the fictions about the River Nile from Passage **B**. Examples have been provided for you.

Facts

essential to support life

_____

_____

_____

_____

_____

_____

_____

_____

Fictions

belongs to the god Isis

_____

_____

_____

_____

_____

_____

_____

_____

11 List the similarities and differences between the Nile and the Amazon from Passages **A** and **B**.

Similarities

very long

_____

_____

_____

_____

_____

_____

_____

_____

Differences

Amazon carries more water

_____

_____

_____

_____

_____

_____

_____

_____

G Directed writing

12   Imagine you have just returned from a cruise on the River Nile. Write a letter to your travel agent to complain that you were disappointed because it did not live up to your expectations. Use information and ideas from Passage **B** in your letter.

_____

_____

_____

_____

_____

_____

_____

_____

_____

_____

_____

_____

_____

_____

_____

_____

_____

_____

_____

_____

_____

_____

_____

_____

_____

_____

_____

_____

_____

_____

_____

_____

_____

_____

_____

_____

H Composition

Descriptive writing

a Describe a busy harbour.

Include as many senses as possible, and think about the following:

- The setting, and the time of day/year and the weather
- The kind of vessels you can see, and what they are doing
- The kind of people you can see, and what they are doing.

b Think of a place you have always wanted to visit. Describe how you see it in your imagination.

Include the following ideas, with supporting detailed description:

- What and where is the place?
- How did you get to know about it and what do you know about it?
- What is it about it that you are attracted to?

Narrative writing

c 'The quest'. Write a story with this title.

You could try the following structure, and end on a cliff-hanger:

- Start in the middle of a situation and refer to the characters.
- Convey information about their search through what they are doing and saying.
- End with them seeing/finding something which may be what they are seeking.

d 'Towards evening, they finally disembarked, but the place was not at all what they had been expecting.' Continue this story.

Answer the following questions:

- Where exactly did they arrive, and what had they been expecting?
- How was the place different, and why?
- What happened after they arrived / how were they received?

Unit 6: Elephant tales

A Reading

1   Read the article below.

Passage A: The artistic elephant

An elephant called Noppakhao, also known as Peter, has painted dozens of works over the last few years, some of them **fetching** as much as $700. He has a delicate brushstroke, a deliberate and <u>controlled</u> style, and an eye for colour that would give Picasso a run for his money. He paints pictures of other elephants, landscapes and flowers, <u>preferring</u> to paint from life rather than to <u>produce</u> abstract works. His most recent painting is a self-portrait.

Noppakhao – whose name <u>translates</u> as 'nine colours of the gemstones' – lives in Ayutthaya province in Thailand. He was <u>introduced</u> to painting eight years ago as part of the Asian Elephant Art & Conservation Project (AEACP), and the purpose of his artistic **endeavours** is to raise money for his **keep** and that of the 90 other elephants on the site, as well as for the training of caretakers. He works with his [1]*mahout*, Mr Pipat Salamgam.

He is a popular and <u>extrovert</u> elephant who loves fun and being the centre of attention. According to his keepers, the 11-year-old bull elephant <u>exhibits</u> a wonderful sense of **dexterity** with the paintbrush. His *mahout* <u>replenishes</u> his brush with paint, but all the movements he makes with it grasped in his trunk are his own. The 'canvas' is paper produced from elephant dung, which is beautifully textured, odourless, and environmentally **sound**.

In the past, elephant painting has led to accusations that the animals are harshly treated in efforts to train them. However, the AEACP insists it does not **tolerate** any abuse of the elephants, either while painting or in everyday <u>interaction</u>. It says: 'We **strive** to give as many elephants as we can a happy, healthy, <u>enriched</u> existence. Money raised by the AEACP is used to provide **captive** elephants with better food, improved shelter and proper veterinary care.'

[1] elephant keeper

47

B Language and style

2   Find replacement words for the following, in the context in which they are used in Passage **A**. The first one has been done for you as an example.

a   fetching _raising_

b   endeavours _____

c   keep _____

d   dexterity _____

e   sound _____

f   tolerate _____

g   strive _____

h   captive _____

3   Judging from the underlined words in the passage, what do the following prefixes mean? Give two more examples of words beginning with each prefix. The first one has been done for you as an example.

a   con- _together, for example 'connect', 'conflict'_

b   pre- _____

c   pro- _____

d   trans- _____

e   intr- _____

f   extr- _____

g   ex- _____

h   re- _____

i   inter- _____

j   en- _____

4   What is the number associated with the following words? Look up any that you don't know. The first one has been done for you as an example.

a   thrice _three_

b   duet _____

c   December _____

d   hexagonal _____

e   pentagon _____

f   binary _____

g   universal _____

h   quadruple _____

i   fortnight _____

j   trinity _____

k   September _____

l   monopoly _____

C Comprehension and summary

5   Select the facts from Passage **A** that are relevant, put them into a suitable order, then write a news report with the headline 'Elephant Picasso paints self-portrait!'

_____

_____

_____

_____

_____

_____

_____

_____

_____

_____

_____

_____

_____

_____

_____

_____

_____

_____

_____

_____

_____

_____

_____

_____

_____

_____

_____

_____

_____

_____

_____

D Directed writing

6 Imagine that you visited the (AEACP) Asian Elephant Art & Conservation project and watched
   the elephant painting. Using and developing information from Passage A, write a journal entry
   about the experience, including what you thought and felt.

_____

_____

_____

_____

_____

_____

_____

_____

_____

_____

_____

_____

_____

_____

_____

_____

_____

_____

_____

_____

_____

_____

_____

_____

_____

E Reading

7   Read the fable below.

Passage B: The elephant and the blind men

Once upon a time, in a faraway land, there lived six blind men. They were friends, but each of them thought himself very wise, much wiser than the others.

One day these six wise blind men went for a walk in a zoo. They could not see the animals but they wanted to listen to them, and they were especially interested in the elephant, of which they had heard much.

That day the zoo-keeper had forgotten to lock the gate of the elephant's cage. Elephants are naturally very curious animals, so it immediately pushed the gate to the cage to see if it might open. To its great delight, it swung wide and the elephant was able to stroll through. Just at that moment the six blind men were passing the elephant's cage. One of them heard a twig snap and went over to see what it was that was walking nearby.

'Greetings!' said the first blind man to the elephant. 'Could you please tell us the way to the elephant enclosure?' The elephant made no noise, but it shifted its weight from left to right, and rocked backwards and forwards. The first blind man walked over to see if this big silent person needed any help. With a bump, he walked right into the side of the elephant. He put out his arms to either side, but all he could feel was the unyielding body of the elephant stretching away in both directions. The first blind man said to the others, 'I think I must have walked into a wall. That's the only explanation.'

The second blind man joined the first. He took up a position to the front of the elephant and grabbed hold of the animal's trunk. He quickly let go of it and shouted, 'Don't be ridiculous. This isn't a wall. This is a snake! We should keep away in case it's poisonous.'

The third man didn't believe either of the other two and decided to find out for himself what it was. He walked to the rear of the elephant and touched its tail. He laughed and said, 'This is neither a wall or a snake. You are both wrong once again. It is quite clear that this is a rope.'

The fourth man knew how opinionated and stubborn his friends could be, always claiming that they were right and the others wrong. He took it upon himself to give his verdict and settle the matter. He crouched down and felt around the bottom of one of the elephant's legs. 'My dear friends,' explained the fourth man, 'this is neither a wall nor a snake. It is no rope either. What we have here, gentlemen, is a tree trunk. That's all there is to say. Let's move on.'

The fifth man had become impatient by now and he realised that it was up to him to pronounce definitively upon the matter. He walked up to the front side of the elephant and felt one of the animal's long tusks. 'What I am holding is long and curved and sharp at the end. It must be a spear. It is not safe to stay here.'

The sixth blind man was by now very puzzled that so many and such different answers could have been given by his five friends. He walked up to the front side of the elephant and grabbed something huge which flapped. He dismissed the other explanations and stated categorically that what they had found was a fan.

The six erstwhile friends began arguing with each other, each maintaining that they alone were right and justifying their opinion. They became very aggressive about it, and started insulting each other.

The zoo-keeper heard the noise the men were making, ran to where they were, and took hold of the escaped elephant, speaking gently to it. The sixth blind man called out, 'Could you please help us? My friends and I do not seem able to figure out what this nearby object is. One of us thinks it's a wall; one thinks it's a snake; one thinks it's a rope; one thinks it's four tree trunks; one thinks it's a sharp weapon. We are in danger of seriously falling out about this matter. Which of us is right, and how can one thing seem so different to six people?'

'Well,' said the zoo-keeper, 'you are all right. And you are all wrong. This is an elephant, but because you each encountered only a part of it, none of you were able to recognise what it really is.'

F Language and style

8 Without looking at Passage **B** again until you have finished the exercise, write out the following extract from it with all the necessary punctuation added.

my dear friends explained the fourth man this is neither a wall nor a snake it is no rope either what we have here gentlemen is four tree trunks thats all there is to say lets move on

_____

_____

_____

_____

_____

G Comprehension and summary

9 a Write the moral of the story, using your own words.

_____

_____

_____

_____

_____

b Rewrite the story in a shorter version, using not more than 150 words (Passage **B** is 762 words).

_____

_____

_____

_____

_____

_____

_____

_____

_____

_____

_____

_____

_____

_____

_____

_____

_____

_____

_____

_____

_____

_____

_____

_____

_____

H Composition

Descriptive writing

a Describe an animal you have seen in its natural habitat, giving details of its appearance and its behaviour at that time.

- Decide where and when you saw the animal, in reality or imaginatively.
- Give details about the environment.
- Use figurative language to convey what it looked like and how it moved.

b Describe the experience of seeing a person or an animal performing an extraordinary feat.

- Where and when you had this real or imagined experience
- What exactly was happening and what was so surprising about the performance
- What you thought and felt as you were watching.

Narrative writing

c Write a story set in a zoo or wildlife park.

- What will be the plot and the ending?
- Who/what are the characters?
- What kind of opening will you use?

d Write a story in which the main character is blind.

- What role will blindness play in the story?
- At what stage will you reveal that they are blind?
- What kind of ending will you use?

Unit 7: Bricks and stones

A Reading

1 Read the article below.

Passage A: Lost marbles

For 200 years there has been a bitter argument between Greece and Britain over the ownership of the Elgin marbles. The issue raises high passions and poses difficult political, legal, moral and cultural questions with far-reaching implications. Although nearly half of the Britons **polled** had no opinion on the matter, 40% of the other half were in favour of returning the marbles to Greece. Greeks are, of course, **unanimous** in their demand.

Dedicated to the goddess Athena, protector of Athens, the marble panels adorning the sacred temple of the Parthenon were removed in August 1801 under the orders of the Earl of Elgin, British Ambassador to the Ottoman Empire, who was a keen collector of antiquities. He intended to use them to decorate his stately home in Scotland. In 1816, they were bought by the British Museum in London. The frieze dates from the time of Pericles, who was the ruler of Athens in the 5th century BCE during its golden age of democracy, philosophy and the arts, a period which was of **profound** and lasting importance for the civilisation of Europe. The carvings show scenes of struggle between men, gods, centaurs and giants, echoing recent battles. They were sculpted by Phidias, who is regarded as the greatest artist of the ancient world.

Much damage was caused to the temple by the removal of the *metopes* (carved panels), when they began a **perilous** journey which took some of the marbles to the bottom of the sea. One shipload of marbles on board a British ship which was travelling to Scotland was caught in a storm and sank near the Greek island

of Kythera. It took two years to salvage the marbles and bring them to the surface.

Since the alleged original document of sale has not been located, no one knows whether Lord Elgin had paid for them in the first place, except for the necessary bribes and site licences; certainly he does not seem to have had permission to remove sculptures still attached to the temple. Lord Byron, who strongly objected to their removal from Greece, **denounced** Elgin as a vandal. Another of his contemporaries, the Romantic poet John Keats, saw them exhibited in London and he was inspired to write two sonnets about them.

Those in favour of the return of the marbles believe they should be reunited with other Greek sculptures in sight of the building that they once adorned, a move for which there is worldwide public support.

The Greeks, who have been seeking the return of the marbles since 1829, when their country became independent, view them as an **intrinsic** part of their national identity and culture, as the essence of Greekness. They have offered various guarantees for the return of their treasures: providing a temperature-controlled, world-class museum to house and display them; paying the cost of their transport to Athens; donating other pieces in a reciprocal exchange; and accepting them as a long-term loan, without transference of ownership. Fragments of the marbles have already been returned by other countries, including the USA. Supporters also point out that Aboriginal ancestral human remains were returned to Tasmania after a 20-year battle with Australia, despite the existence of the British Museum charter preventing the repatriation of items in its collection.

Those who resist the demand for the restitution of the marbles point out that they would not have survived at all had they remained in Athens, and that Lord Elgin saved them for **posterity**. The city fell to Byzantines, Franks and Turks, and the Parthenon was damaged by fire and earthquake as recently as 1981.

In 1687, during a siege, the Turkish garrison's gunpowder stored inside the Parthenon was ignited, bringing down walls and columns, and the Acropolis was twice besieged during the Greek War of Independence in the 1820s. The Venetians shattered the horses of Athena and Poseidon while they were trying to remove them, and other pieces had been carried off to the Louvre museum in Paris before Elgin's 'theft' and relocation of the marbles in 1801.

However, while the artefacts held in London may have been saved from the hazards of war, they suffered gravely from 19th-century pollution and were **irrevocably** damaged by cleaning methods employed by British Museum staff, which destroyed the original fine detail of the carving.

The British Museum continues to resist political pressure and intends to hold on to its prize exhibits. Officials claim that the return of the marbles to Greece would open the floodgates to all countries wanting their antiquities back, and the world's museums and libraries would have to **dismantle** their collections and close down, thereby **diminishing** their own nation's educational and financial resources. Tourist attractions would be rendered national rather than international, which, they argue, would be a retrograde step, as links and comparisons between the world's greatest artefacts can only be possible in international exhibitions. Since more than half the original marbles are lost, the return of the ones in Britain would not complete the collection.

The Museum takes the view that history cannot be rewound and that by displaying the marbles in London – and by not charging for entry – the Museum has spread the culture of classical Greek civilisation, which has been an inspiration to generations of people of all nationalities.

> *frieze*: a decorated band along the upper part of a wall

B Language and style

2 Give single words or phrases as synonyms for the following words from Passage A.

a polled _surveyed_

f intrinsic _____

b unanimous _____

g posterity _____

c profound _____

h irrevocably _____

d perilous _____

i dismantle _____

e denounced _____

j diminishing _____

3 Underline all the words beginning with *re* in Passage A. Write down those which are the correct synonyms for the following words or phrases.

a joined again _reunited_

f turned back _____

b taken away _____

g change of place _____

c in return _____

h return to country of origin _____

d oppose _____

i moving backwards _____

e return to owner _____

j supplies _____

4 Using different colours for each tense, underline or highlight in Passage A all the verbs in the four **past tenses**: *present perfect, simple past, past continuous, past perfect*. **Fill in the gaps below to explain their usage.**

For a completed and dated action in the past we use the _____, whereas for an action which began in the past but which is not yet completed, we use the _____. The past perfect tense is used when an action _____. The past continuous shows that an action was _____ when _____.

5 Circle all the uses of *which* and *who* in Passage A. Notice that when followed by a comma, they are adding separate information about the noun; when there is no comma, they are part of the definition of the noun. Join the simple sentences below into one complex sentence by using *which* or *who*, and a comma if necessary.

a I visited the exhibition. I heard about it on the radio.

I visited the exhibition, which I heard about on the radio.

b I read about the man. He had stolen the statues.

_____

c I bought a book. It was about the history of Greece.

_____

d I met Lord Byron. He had written a poem the previous day.

_____

e We have not visited Greece. We have heard it is a beautiful country.

f   I spoke to a woman in the gallery. She was the one I had met previously.

_____

g   It is difficult to find the people. They are responsible for the damage.

_____

h   This is the Museum Director. He is against the return of the marbles.

_____

i   They didn't find the sculpture. It was buried by an earthquake.

_____

j   You should have interviewed Lord Elgin. I introduced him to you.

_____

C Comprehension and summary

6   **a**   What percentage of Greeks want the marbles returned to Greece?

_____

b   How did some of the marbles end up on the sea bed?

_____

c   Who had a 20-year battle with Australia?

_____

d   What caused damage to the marbles?

_____

e   What were the responses by Elgin's contemporaries to the marbles being displayed in London?

_____

7   **Use the information in Passage A to write a dialogue between a British Museum official and a representative of the Greek Ministry of Culture, who argue about who should have custody of the Elgin marbles.**

MC: I must insist on behalf of the Greek people that this important part of our cultural heritage is returned to where it belongs.

BM: _____

_____

_____

_____

_____

_____

(lines for writing)

D Directed writing

8   Write a letter to the editor of a national newspaper, giving your view on whether or not cultural artefacts should be returned to their country of origin.

(lines for writing)

E Reading

9   Read the article below.

Passage B: High water

Every winter Venice fears the *acqua alta*, which threatens to **overwhelm** it; **relentless** high tides are eating into the wooden doors and shutters of ground-floor apartments. No one lives on the ground floor any more and Venetians are leaving their drowning home; the population has **dwindled** by 100000 in 50 years to 70000. The worst thing about the floods is their **unpredictability**, and that they cost the city $5 million annually in lost working hours. **Priceless** frescoes are subject to damp and are at risk of permanent water damage; tourists find they have wet feet in St Mark's Square 50 times a year. This flooding is most **dramatic** when a higher-than-average tide **coincides** with various other **phenomena** – such as heavy rainfall inland from the Venetian lagoon, a wind blowing in from the Adriatic Sea or an area of low pressure.

High water is most likely to occur between September and April, though it's not unheard of at other times. July is just about the only dry month in a city of water built in a lagoon in the Adriatic Sea. If you are a tourist planning ahead, you can expect the highest tides around the time of a full moon or a new moon. When a level above 110 centimetres is expected – which will invade nearly 12% of Venice – sirens will sound a warning 3–4 hours in advance of high tide, with an increasing number of tones to signify every 10 centimetres above 110 centimetres, warning residents to protect their properties and get out their wellington boots. The speakers are concealed inside bell towers and public buildings.

For half a century, there has been constant debate on how to save the city, but no agreement can be reached, not even on whether the situation is getting worse. The number of high tides varies between 80 and 100 in **consecutive** years, without any apparent **trend**; the worst flood of 194 centimetres was in 1966, but in 2001, there was a high tide of 144 centimetres. What is certain is that the Adriatic has risen by 23 centimetres over the last 50 years, after decades of **stability**. This may be due to global factors, or to heavy draining of underground water by local factories; an **aggravating** factor is that the city also suffers from subsidence.

Venice has twin problems of subsidence and rising water levels. The **current** plan to **alleviate** flooding consists of giant gates at the entrances to the lagoon. Many locals believe the development is a waste of money and may even worsen the situation. This remains to be seen, but Venice is certainly one of the world's first major cities to be threatened by rising sea levels due to climate change. Paintings by Venice's most famous artist, Canaletto, show how much the sea has risen around the city in the years since his death in 1768: 80 centimetres, an average of 2.4 millimetres annually. His paintings are so realistic that they include tidemarks on the buildings beside canals.

When the tide is high, the boats cannot pass under the bridges, and kilometres of temporary raised wooden walkways (*passerelle*) have to be laid to keep feet dry, though these are in danger of being swept away by the high waters and there are particular fears for schoolchildren. Barriers are finally being installed on the sea-bed of the lagoon, but after 15 years of building they are still not completed. In the meantime, an additional cause of damage is the regular visits to the city by giant cruise vessels, which sail along the Grand Canal, creating water displacement and pollution.

F Language and style

10 Use the following words, shown in bold in Passage **B**, in sentences of your own which show you understand their meaning. Look up any that you are not sure of.

a overwhelm *The intense heat threatened to overwhelm him.*

b relentless

c dwindled

d unpredictability

e priceless

f dramatic

g coincides

h phenomena

i consecutive

j trend

k stability

l aggravating

m current

n alleviate

11 Add **prepositions** in the spaces below, then check back in Passage **B** to see whether your answers are correct. The first one has been done for you as an example.

 a eating *into*_____ the wooden doors

 b the worst thing _____ the floods

 c subject _____ damp

 d at risk _____ permanent water damage

 e debate _____ how to save

 f suffers _____ subsidence

 g in danger _____ being swept away

12 Study the use of full stops, semi-colons and commas in the first paragraph of Passage **B**, then fill in the missing **punctuation** marks in the next two paragraphs, copied below, without looking back until you have finished.

> High water is most likely to occur between September and April though its not unheard of at other times July is just about the only dry month in a city of water built in a lagoon in the Adriatic Sea. If you are a tourist planning ahead you can expect the highest tides around the time of a full moon or a new moon. When a level above 110 centimeters is expected which will invade nearly 12% of Venice sirens will sound a warning 3–4 hours in advance of high tide with an increasing number of tones to signify every 10 centimeters above 110 centimeters warning residents to protect their properties and get out their wellington boots. The speakers are concealed inside bell towers and public buildings.
>
> For half a century there has been constant debate on how to save the city but no agreement can be reached not even on whether the situation is getting worse. The number of high tides varies between 80 and 100 in consecutive years without any apparent trend the worst flood of 194 centimeters was in 1966 but in 2001 there was a high tide of 144 centimeters. What is certain is that the Adriatic has risen by 23 centimeters over the last 50 years after decades of stability. This may be due to global factors or to heavy draining of underground water by local factories an aggravating factor is that the city also suffers from subsidence.

G Comprehension and summary

13 **a** Which words and phrases does the writer of Passage **B** use to convey the seriousness of the threats to Venice of the high tides?

_____

_____

_____

_____

_____

_____

b Which words and phrases does the writer of Passage **B** use to convey the difficulty of finding a solution to the problem?

_____

_____

_____

_____

_____

_____

H Directed writing

14 Imagine that you live in Venice. Write a speech to be delivered at a public meeting which demands that something be done about the effect the water levels are having on your own life and that of the city.

_____

_____

_____

_____

_____

_____

_____

_____

_____

_____

_____

_____

_____

_____

_____

_____

_____

_____

_____

_____

_____

_____

_____

_____

_____

_____

_____

I Composition

Descriptive writing

a Describe a large public building, such as a castle, palace or hotel, which made a strong impression on you when you visited it. Use a spatial structure.

- Approach the building and describe its exterior, noticing more details as you get closer.
- Enter the building and describe the entrance and your first impressions.
- Go further into building/upstairs and describe a room, the furniture/decor, and the view through the window.

b Describe the scenery, and your thoughts and feelings, when you arrive in a country you are visiting for the first time. Use a spatial structure.

- What do you see and hear as you are driven from the airport to the city?
- What are the sights and sounds on the city streets as you get closer to the centre?
- What can you see from your hotel room, including what people are doing in the street below?

Narrative writing

c 'I looked back, and saw that the building was now just a heap of rubble.' Write a story with this as the last sentence.

- Think of an idea for a story which would fit this title (from a book or film).
- Plan your characters, including the first person narrator and where you will use dialogue.
- Decide on a suitable opening sentence, which refers to the building.

d Write a story that involves a stolen or fake work of art, beginning with 'I had no idea when I first saw it that it was going to cause such trouble.'

- Think of an idea for a story which would fit this title (from a book or film).
- Plan your characters, including the first person narrator and where you will use dialogue.
- Decide on as suitable closing sentence, which refers to the work of art.

Unit 8: Aiming high

A Reading

1   Read the article below, which has gaps at the beginning of some of the sentences.

Passage A: Full of hot air

The first passengers of a hot air balloon, on September 19th 1783, were a sheep, a duck and a rooster. They came crashing to the ground after 15 minutes. A couple of months later, the first manned attempt took place in a balloon made by the French Montgolfier brothers. It flew for a period of 20 minutes from its launch in the centre of Paris. Two years later, the first flight across the English Channel took place, which was considered the first significant step in ballooning history. (1)_____, the attempt to **replicate** the journey resulted in the death of the balloonist due to the use of a hydrogen balloon *in tandem with* a helium balloon. (2)_____, George Washington saw the launch of the first hot air balloon in North America in 1793.
   (3)_____, at this time hot air balloons were hailed as the future of travel. It was believed that they **epitomised** freedom and symbolised prosperity, and that these *commodities* could be carried across the globe, **denying *national frontiers* and defying *territorial boundaries.***
   (4)_____, ***the balloon dream deflated*** in the following century, mostly as a result of the series of horrendous accidents which *ensued*. They were not, in fact, any good at all for travel, as they couldn't be steered, so they soon became a form of entertainment instead: acrobats hung from them (and often fell); fireworks were set off from them (often **catastrophically**). Napoleon saw them as a potential weapon of war, but was *disabused* of this belief when Nelson **wiped out** his balloon regiment in the Battle of the Nile in 1794. (5)_____, balloons were used in the American Civil War to advise ground troops about enemy positions. (6)_____, there was briefly a balloon postal service during the Prussian siege of Paris in 1870, taking mail and homing pigeons to the outside world.

   Notwithstanding the previous disasters, they have proved useful in research into insect airflows and therefore bird migration paths, and in determining how high humans can go and survive in the ever-decreasing amounts of oxygen in the stratosphere. (7)_____, they continued to pose a challenge for record breakers, and not only for the fictional characters of Jules Verne adventure novels. Three Swedish aeronauts attempted to reach the North Pole by balloon in 1897; their *remains* were not discovered until 1930.

   British billionaire Richard Branson and Swedish engineer Per Lindstrand completed the first transatlantic hot-air balloon flight in the Virgin Atlantic Flyer in 1987, and four years later they broke the manned-balloon altitude record when over Texas at almost 20 000 metres while on a 8000-kilometre Pacific crossing from Japan to Canada lasting 46 hours. This has since been beaten by Dr Vijaypat Singhania of India, who recorded the height of 21 027 metres in a Cameron Z-1600 hot-air balloon over Mumbai on 26th November 2005.

   Going with the wind remains appealing to this day, and buying someone a trip in a hot air balloon continues to be a popular choice of birthday present – at least for the purchaser.

B Language and style

2 Insert the following discourse markers/paragraph links in the appropriate places in the blanks in Passage **A** and note which number blank you are matching them with.

moreover; consequently; in addition; nevertheless; unfortunately; nonetheless; however

3 Give the **noun** form of the following words from the passage.

a replicate _____

b epitomised _____

c catastrophically _____

d denying _____

e defying _____

4 Give synonyms for:

a commodities _____

b ensued _____

c disabused _____

d notwithstanding _____

e remains _____

C Comprehension and summary

5 Comment on the devices and effects of the following phrases in italics in Passage **A**.

a *in tandem with*

_____

b *denying national frontiers and defying territorial boundaries*

_____

c *the balloon dream deflated*

_____

d *wiped out*

_____

e *Going with the wind*

_____

6 Re-read Passage **A**. Write a summary of:

a Ways in which hot air ballooning has failed to live up to expectations

_____

_____

_____

_____

_____

_____

_____

_____

_____
_____
_____
_____
_____
_____

b Ways in which hot air ballooning has continued to be appealing

_____
_____
_____
_____
_____
_____
_____
_____
_____
_____
_____
_____
_____
_____

D Directed writing

7   Write a journal entry as one of the balloonists referred to in Passage **A**. You may develop ideas from the text, add inferences, and make up factual material of your own to include in your record of part of your flight.

_____
_____
_____
_____

E Reading

8   Read the internet news article below.

Passage B: Over the top proposal

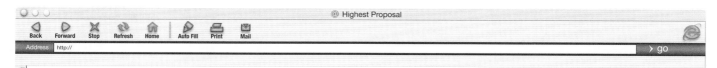

There are many creative and romantic ways to propose. However, one Malaysian dare devil went above and beyond to show his girlfriend just how much she means to him.

Keow Wee Loong, 28, decided to put his climbing skills to good use by scaling the world's tallest bridge (550 metres) in China to propose to his girlfriend.

He filmed the whole stunt and took pictures before posting it on her Facebook page to pop the question on 27th November 2016.

The couple met back in May 2016, while Loong was in Japan to take photos inside the Fukushima exclusion zone, when he lost his wallet containing 300,000 yen (roughly $2,600). He then stumbled into a Family Mart convenience store where he met his now fiancée Marta Sibielak, 24, from Poland.

At the time, Sibielak was preparing curry for a customer and greeted Loong in Japanese. When he replied back in English, she lit up.

'She spoke to me in Japanese, assuming I was Japanese. But I replied to her in English and she seemed excited to be able to speak to a foreigner,' Loong reported.

After she treated him to a bowl of curry, the two talked for over an hour. Loong grew fond of his new friend and wanted to get her contact info.

He was hesitant at first because he was shy and was scared she had a boyfriend. However, he knew he couldn't miss this rare opportunity.

'I knew if I didn't ask for her contact number, I would never see her again,' he said.

For the next four days up until he had to go to Fukushima, Loong visited Sibielak at work every day and walked her back home after work. Sometimes he'd miss the train and had to walk two hours back to his hotel.

Six months later, Loong decided to pop the question, but wanted it to be extra special. He decided to film himself on the tallest building in China and show her the video. However, he was caught by security so decided to change locations to Beipanjiang Bridge, the world's tallest bridge.

Loon and his videographer Abraham Shilton Cambala spent over two hours climbing the mountain to the bridge — and another 40 minutes scaling to the top of the crane, 740-metres high.

'It was cold and strong wind caused the crane to wobble. We had limited time to get the footage we needed and the spot I was standing in was easily visible by security below.'

Loong took Sibielak to a trip in Bali, Indonesia. While they were eating at a restaurant, Loong excused himself to go to the bathroom. Knowing she always checks Facebook whenever she's waiting for someone, he uploaded the following photo.

Sibielak was the first person to comment and replied with a simple 'yes'.

By the time Loong came back from the bathroom, she was crying tears of joy. Shortly after, he presented her with the engagement ring on Kuta beach in Bali.

Currently the two are in a long distance relationship, but plan to get married next year. They will start their new life in Malaysia after Sibielak finishes her studies in Japan.

Article used with permissions from Netshark.com

69

F Language and style

9 **a** How you can tell from the vocabulary and syntax of Passage **B** that it is an informal text?

_____

_____

_____

_____

_____

_____

_____

b How can you tell from the structure of Passage **B** that it is a news report?

_____

_____

_____

_____

_____

10 **a** List the initial time adverbials used in the passage.

_____

_____

_____

_____

_____

_____

_____

_____

b What purposes do they serve?

_____

_____

_____

_____

G Comprehension and summary

11 Put these 12 events in the order in which they occurred by putting a number next to each. The first one had been indicated for you.

she accepted the proposal

he lost his wallet (l)

they met in a shop

she gave him a free curry

he went to Fukushima

they went to Bali

he returned to Malaysia

he visited her at work

he climbed the bridge

he was caught by security

he sent her a photo

they got engaged

12 Imagine you are Sibielak. In two paragraphs tell the story from your point of view.

_____

_____

_____

_____

_____

_____

_____

_____

_____

_____

_____

_____

_____

_____

_____

_____

_____

_____

H Directed writing

13 Restructure the information given in Passage **B** and rewrite it as a news report, in a different style. Give it a headline.

_____

_____

_____

_____

_____

_____

_____

_____

_____

_____

_____

_____

_____

_____

_____

_____

_____

_____

_____

_____

_____

_____

_____

_____

_____

_____

_____

_____

_____

_____

_____

_____

_____

_____

_____

_____

_____

_____

_____

_____

I Composition

Descriptive writing

a Write a description entitled 'Looking down'. Imagine you are high up and describe what you can see below.

- Choose a place, e.g. a tall building or a plane, and describe the kind of landscape that lies below.
- Give details of what can be seen, describing precise shapes and colours.
- What do you think and feel about being so high up?

b Describe the moment when you are told about a surprise, e.g. a birthday party or holiday.

- Who are you, who are you with, and where are you when the surprise is announced?
- What is the exact nature of the surprise and what is your reaction to the person who announces it?
- What are you really thinking and feeling?

Narrative writing

c 'As they ascended in the high speed lift, he realised that he really didn't want to be here after all …' Continue this story.

- Why is he in a lift, who is with him, what is waiting at the top?
- How and why did he get into this situation?
- What happens next and how does it end?

d Write a story of someone who wants to impress someone.

- Who are they, and who do they want to impress, and why?
- What do they decide to do?
- What happens next and how does it end?

Unit 9: In deep water

A Reading

1 Read the article below.

Passage A: The cave

Caving is a madness. Any sensible person can see this. The idea of squeezing through cracks and fissures, abseiling into deep, dark holes, pulling yourself through 12-centimetre crawl spaces by your fingers and toes because you can't get enough of an angle to use your knees and elbows is all horrifyingly claustrophobic enough. But getting stuck halfway through, rock above pressing down on your back, rock below pressing up on your chest? It's the geological equivalent of an anaconda's embrace. Panic only makes things worse.

Deep-water diving is equally insane. Humans just aren't designed to survive under the immense weight of water. At any significant depth, the oxygen in air becomes poisonous and the nitrogen becomes narcotic. To adapt, divers must 'water down' the air with helium. They must do this at exactly the right time. Get it wrong and they risk horrible side effects, such as vomiting, amnesia, seizures and worse. The deeper they go, the smaller the margins for error. Any miscalculations, equipment malfunctions or unknowns and they can't simply swim to safety. Gas in the blood stream has to be released slowly to avoid 'the bends'. The bends are bad. And, of course, panic only makes things worse.

Cave-diving combines these two unfathomable pastimes. It offers all the associated horrors of clambering through inhospitable nooks and crannies with all the complexities of being under water. It is routinely described as one of the most dangerous sports on the planet, but unlike all the other contenders for this accolade – proximity flying, base jumping, rodeo-riding and so forth – it is not an adrenaline sport. Cruelly, your safety depends on remaining relaxed. Pulse rates must never quicken. Breathing must never shorten. Zen-like calm is essential, particularly in situations where you don't feel calm at all. What you want is nice and boring. Under water, things happen slowly. If a parachute fails on a base jump, you have seconds to contemplate your fate. If something goes wrong 10 kilometres down an underwater tunnel, you usually have only until your air runs out to find a solution or make your peace.

There were plenty of quite large incidents in the pioneering days of the sport. Before technical advances during the Second World War, you had two options if you wanted to swim through a submerged cave. Option A, you could hold your breath, dive in and hope there was a pocket of air on the other side. Option B, you could invest in the very latest technology – standard diving equipment consisting of a brass helmet and an unwieldy waterproof suit. Option A was risky but Option B had its downsides, too. It required an air supply to be fed through from the surface.

Even with the advent of self-contained breathing apparatus, the sport was hardly unhazardous. Deaths came with faulty equipment, overzealous ambition and, most of all, problems with orientation. Many cave-diving fatalities have occurred when divers kick up silt, lose their way in zero visibility and then run out of air. To reduce the risk, cave-divers follow a guide line (or lay new line if the cave is undiscovered.)

Equipment has improved a lot since the early days, but accidents still happen. Those who do this sport can't stop because they have to know what's around the next corner, even if it is just another tunnel.

From an article by Mat Rudd, *The Sunday Times*, 1st December 2013.

B Language and style

2 Write crossword clues for the words below from Passage **A**, which are the answers, bearing in mind the part of speech, e.g. sensible – possessed of ability to be rational. You may need to use a dictionary.

a claustrophobic _____

_____

b narcotic _____

_____

c contenders _____

_____

d accolade _____

_____

e pioneering _____

_____

3 These are crossword clues. Find the synonymous words in Passage **A** which could be the answers.

a failures to work properly _____

b cumbersome or awkward to manage _____

c arrival of something/someone bringing change _____

d excessively keen _____

e directional awareness _____

4 a Identify the binomial pair (a fixed-order phrase of two synonymous words joined by 'and') and the simile in paragraph 1.

_____

b Identify the binomial pair and the pun usage in paragraph 3.

_____

C Comprehension and summary

5 a Select words and phrases from paragraph 1 which show the writer's attitude to caving.

_____

_____

b Select words and phrases from paragraph 2 which show the writer's attitude to diving.

_____

_____

    c Summarise in one sentence of your own words what the writer feels about cave-diving.

_____

_____

6 Make two lists of notes, one each for the dangers of underwater cave exploration and of deep-water diving.

Dangers of underwater cave exploration	**Dangers of deep-water diving**
narrow cracks	*poisonous oxygen*

D Directed writing

7 Using the information in Passage **A**, write an encyclopedia entry under the heading of 'Cave diving'.

E Reading

8   Read the following extract.

Passage B: Men overboard!

My first concern was to look for the ship. I glimpsed a black mass disappearing eastward, its lights fading in the distance. I shouted for help, swimming desperately toward the *Abraham Lincoln*. My clothes were weighing me down. I was sinking! Then I found and seized the arm of my loyal friend.

'What about the ship?' I asked.

'As I jumped overboard, I heard the helmsman shout, 'Our propeller and rudder are smashed by the monster's tusk!''

'Then the ship can no longer steer, and we are done for!'

Having concluded that our sole chance for salvation lay in being picked up by the ship's longboats, we had to take steps to wait for them as long as possible. I decided to divide our energies so we wouldn't both be worn out at the same time: while one of us lay on his back, the other would swim and propel his partner forward.

The monster had rammed us at 11 in the evening. I therefore calculated on eight hours of swimming until sunrise. The dense gloom was broken only by the phosphorescent flickers coming from our movements. I stared at the luminous ripples breaking over my hands, shimmering sheets spattered with blotches of bluish grey. It seemed as if we'd plunged into a pool of quicksilver.

An hour later, I was overcome with tremendous exhaustion. My limbs stiffened in the grip of intense cramps and paralysing cold. I tried to call out. My swollen lips wouldn't let a single sound through. I heard my friend cry 'Help!'. Ceasing all movement for an instant, we listened. His shout had received an answer. I could barely hear it. I was at the end of my strength; my fingers gave out; my mouth opened convulsively, filling with brine …

Just then something hard banged against me. I clung to it and was pulled back to the surface. I fainted … then someone was shaking me vigorously.

'Ned!' I exclaimed. 'You were thrown overboard after the collision?'

'Yes, professor, but I was luckier than you and immediately able to set foot on our gigantic whale. I soon realized why my harpoon got blunted and couldn't puncture its hide. This beast is made of plated steel!'

I hoisted myself to the summit of this half-submerged creature that was serving as our refuge. I tested it with my foot. Obviously it was some hard, impenetrable substance; not the soft matter that makes up the bodies of our big marine mammals but a bony carapace, like those that covered some prehistoric animals. The blackish back supporting me was smooth and polished with no overlapping scales. On impact, it gave off a metallic resonance and, incredibly, it seemed to be made of riveted plates. No doubts were possible! This animal, this monster, this natural phenomenon that had puzzled the whole scientific world, that had muddled and misled the minds of sailors, was an even more astonishing one – made by the hand of man! There was no question now. We were stretched out on the back of some kind of underwater boat that took the form of an immense steel fish.

Just then, a bubbling began astern and the boat started to move. We barely had time to hang on to its topside, which emerged about 80 centimetres above water. It was imperative to make contact with whatever beings were confined inside the machine. I searched its surface for an opening, but the lines of rivets were straight and uniform. Moreover, the moon then disappeared and left us in profound darkness. We would have to wait for daylight to find some way of getting inside this underwater boat, and if it made a dive, we were done for!

In the early hours, the vessel picked up speed. We could barely cope with this dizzying rush, and the waves battered us at close range. Our hands came across a ring fastened to its back, and we all held on for dear life. Finally, the long night was over. From inside the boat came noises of iron fastenings pushed aside. One of the steel plates flew up, and a few moments later, eight sturdy fellows appeared silently and dragged us down into their fearsome machine.

This brutally executed capture was carried out with lightning speed. My companions and I had no time to collect ourselves. I don't know how they felt about being shoved inside this aquatic prison, but as for me, I was shivering all over. With whom were we dealing? Surely with some new breed of pirates, exploiting the sea after their own fashion.

From *Twenty Thousand Leagues Under the Sea*, by Jules Verne.

F Language and style

9 **a** Passage **B** contains **adjectives** used to intensify the drama and danger. List them here.

_____ _____

_____ _____

_____ _____

_____ _____

_____ _____

_____ _____

b Comment on the collective effect in the passage of the following verbs:

seized, smashed, rammed _____

_____

_____

_____

c Comment on the collective effect in the passage of the following nouns:

monster, beast, creature _____

_____

_____

_____

10 **Explain using evidence how tension has been created in the narrative through setting and event, structure and tone.**

_____

_____

_____

_____

_____

_____

_____

_____

_____

_____

_____

11 **Punctuate** the paragraph of Passage **B** below, which has had paragraph breaks, inverted commas, commas and semi-colons, apostrophes, question and exclamation marks, and ellipses (triple dots / suspension marks) removed. Use // to show a change of paragraph.

An hour later I was overcome with tremendous exhaustion. My limbs stiffened in the grip of intense cramps and paralysing cold. I tried to call out. My swollen lips wouldnt let a single sound through. I heard my friend cry Help. Ceasing all movement for an instant we listened. His shout had received an answer. I could barely hear it. I was at the end of my strength my fingers gave out my mouth opened convulsively filling with brine Just then something hard banged against me. I clung to it and was pulled back to the surface. I fainted then someone was shaking me vigorously. Ned I exclaimed. You were thrown overboard after the collision Yes professor but I was luckier than you and immediately able to set foot on our gigantic whale. I soon realised why my harpoon got blunted and couldnt puncture its hide. This beast is made of plated steel

G Comprehension and summary

12 Describe the character of the professor, drawing inferences from the way he speaks and behaves in the passage. Give evidence to support your description.

_____

_____

_____

_____

_____

_____

_____

_____

_____

_____

13 Highlight in the passage the points to be included, and then write what happened to the professor between late evening and dawn the following morning, in not more than 250 of your own words.

_____

_____

_____

_____

_____

_____

_____

_____

_____
_____
_____
_____
_____
_____
_____
_____
_____
_____

H Directed writing

14 Write the professor's journal entry for the events described in the passage, focusing on his changing thoughts and feelings about the 'monster'.

_____
_____
_____
_____
_____
_____
_____
_____
_____
_____
_____
_____
_____
_____
_____
_____
_____
_____
_____

_____

_____

_____

_____

_____

_____

_____

_____

_____

_____

_____

_____

I Composition

Descriptive writing

a Describe being trapped on a sinking ship. Use a chronological structure:

- Describe where you are, what has happened, and what you are thinking and feeling as you first realise the situation.
- Describe how the situation has deteriorated after a short period of time has passed, and how your thoughts and feelings have changed.
- Describe how the situation has reached a desperate stage after another short passage of time, and what finally happens.

b Describe a leisure boat trip. Use a spatial structure:

- You are leaving harbour. What can you see, hear and smell?
- Describe the vessel, its occupants and its movement. How do you feel?
- You are approaching land again. What can you see? What are you thinking?

Narrative writing

c Write a story entitled 'A narrow escape'.

- Who are the characters and what situation are they in?
- What is the setting and atmosphere?
- What is the series of speeches and events leading to escape?

d Write a story in which someone pushes themselves beyond their limits.

- Who and where is the main character?
- What is the challenge and why is it dangerous?
- What goes wrong and what are the consequences?

Unit 10: Losing sleep

A Reading

1   **Read the article below.**

Passage A: Night raider

How can something so small cause so much trouble, making the killer instinct arise in us all? Weighing no more than a speck of dust, it _strikes_ before we are even aware of its presence, then wafts off in drunken flight carrying its precious load and singing its high-pitched song of _victory_. Man's public _enemy_ number one – the mosquito.

With its long, streaming legs the mosquito floats in the air, **prowling** for a bare arm or leg to bite and feed upon. Even in the darkness, the insect is surrounded by an aura of **evil** as it seeks to take advantage of the sleeping innocent. And yet, its **malice** goes further, for it not only steals a person's blood and leaves an itchy red bump, but sometimes it also injects malaria – a feared and often fatal disease. Consider the time, trouble and money we spend on fighting this monster. We drape mosquito nets over the bed, we burn mosquito coils, we rub insect repellent into our exposed flesh, we spray aerosol and we swallow anti-malaria pills. We even hunt the creatures all over the room, throwing shoes, pillows

and magazines in a barrage of anti-mosquito fire so that we might put an end to the torment brought about by its infuriating buzzing about our ears. Sometimes we get lucky and spot one of the intruders hovering in the turbulence created by our frantic movements and, as it desperately tries to gain a safe altitude, we manage to squash the hated speck in a stinging clap of execution. Our sense of achievement is short-lived though. As we gaze at the bright smear on our hand, we realise that we are looking at our own blood, recently _plundered_.

How do we put an end to this menace? Perhaps we should learn a lesson from this **fiend** and, in addition to putting up screens and defences, we should move into the attack and invade the mosquito's home. If we spray the stagnant pools of water where the mosquitoes breed and make sure than no containers are left around to collect rain water and so provide them with a new home, perhaps we will be able to outwit the mosquito and sleep soundly in our beds at night without fear of an air raid.

B Language and style

2   **What is the effect of the following in Passage A:**

   a   the title *Night Raider*?

   _____

   _____

   _____

   b   the words in bold?

   _____

   _____

   _____

   c   the underlined words?

   _____

   _____

   _____

   d   the rhetorical questions, imperative sentences and non-sentences?

   _____

   _____

   e   the use of *we* throughout the passage?

   _____

   _____

3   **a**   Explain the difference between the verbs *raise*, *rise* and *arise*.

   _____

   _____

   _____

   b   Give the **simple past** and **past participle** form of each of the verbs in 3a.

   _____

   _____

   _____

   c   Use each of the three verbs in a sentence to demonstrate its meaning.

   _____

   _____

   _____

4   **Fill in the missing prepositions without looking back at Passage A, then check the third paragraph of the passage to see whether you have completed it correctly.**

Consider the time, trouble and money we spend _on_____ fighting this monster. We drape mosquito nets _____ the bed, we burn mosquito coils, we rub insect repellent _____ our exposed flesh, we spray aerosol and we swallow anti-malaria pills. We even hunt the creatures all _____ the room, throwing shoes, pillows and magazines _____ a barrage of anti-mosquito fire so that we might put an end _____ the torment brought about _____ its infuriating buzzing _____our ears. Sometimes we get lucky and spot one of the intruders hovering _____ the turbulence created by our frantic movements and, as it desperately tries _____gain a safe altitude, we manage to squash the hated speck _____a stinging clap _____execution. Our sense of achievement is short-lived though. As we gaze _____the bright smear _____our hand, we realise that we are looking _____our own blood, recently plundered.

5   **The last sentence in Passage A is a conditional sentence. Complete the rules describing the functions and use of tenses of the four types of conditional.**

The first conditional uses the _present simple____tense with the future tense for events which are _____. Second conditionals, which use the simple past followed by _____ plus _____, signify an event which could happen but which is _____. Third conditionals, formed with the _____ tense followed by plus _____ , mean that the event is _____because it _____. There are also zero conditionals, using simple present in both clauses, which refer to _____.

C Comprehension and summary

6   **What other relevant title(s) could you give the passage?**

_____

_____

7   **Make a list of ten points from the passage to explain why the writer hates mosquitoes.**

a   _we are not aware of them until too late_____

b   _____

c   _____

d   _____

e   _____

f   _____

g   _____

h   _____

i   _____

j   _____

85

D Directed writing

8   Write a public health information leaflet, consisting of bullet points in full sentences, for the heading 'Public enemy number one – the mosquito'. Explain in suitable language why and how one needs to protect oneself from mosquitoes.

_____

_____

_____

_____

_____

_____

_____

_____

_____

_____

_____

_____

_____

_____

_____

_____

_____

_____

_____

_____

_____

_____

_____

_____

E Reading

9 **Read the short story extract below.**

Passage B: A terribly strange bed

The extracts from a gothic horror story describe the beginning of the narrator's sleepless night in a hotel.

I soon felt not only that I could not go to sleep, but that I could not even close my eyes. I was wide awake, and in a high fever. Every nerve in my body trembled – every one of my senses seemed to be **preternaturally** sharpened. I tossed and rolled, and tried every kind of position, and **perseveringly** sought out the cold corners of the bed, and all to no purpose. Now I thrust my arms over the clothes; now I poked them under the clothes; now I violently shot my legs straight out down to the bottom of the bed; now I **convulsively** coiled them up as near my chin as they would go; now I shook out my crumpled pillow, changed it to the cool side, patted it flat, and lay down quietly on my back; now I fiercely doubled it in two, set it up on end, thrust it against the board of the bed, and tried a sitting posture. Every effort was in vain; I groaned with **vexation** as I felt that I was in for a sleepless night.

What could I do? I had no book to read. And yet, unless I found out some method of **diverting** my mind, I felt certain that I was in the condition to imagine all sorts of horrors; to rack my brain with **forebodings** of every possible and impossible danger; in short, to pass the night in suffering all conceivable varieties of nervous terror.

I raised myself on my elbow, and looked about the room – which was brightened by a lovely moonlight pouring straight through the window – to see if it contained any pictures or ornaments that I could at all clearly distinguish.

There was, first, the bed I was lying in; a four-post bed, with the regular top lined with chintz – the regular fringed valance all round – the regular stifling, **unwholesome** curtains, which I remembered having mechanically drawn back against the posts without particularly noticing the bed when I first got into the room. Then there was the marble-topped wash-stand, from which the water I had spilled, in my hurry to pour it out, was still dripping, slowly and more slowly, on to the brick floor. Then two small chairs, with my coat, waistcoat, and trousers flung on them [...] Then the dressing-table, **adorned** by a very small looking-glass, and a very large pincushion. Then the window – an unusually large window. Then a dark old picture, which the feeble candle dimly showed me. It was a picture of a fellow in a high Spanish hat, crowned with a plume of towering feathers. A sinister **ruffian**, looking upward, shading his eyes with his hand, and looking intently upward.

This picture put a kind of constraint upon me to look upward too – at the top of the bed. It was a gloomy and not an interesting object, and I looked back at the picture. I counted the feathers in the man's hat – they stood out in relief – three white, two green. I observed the crown of his hat, which was of conical shape, according to the fashion supposed to have been favoured by Guido Fawkes. I wondered what he was looking up at. It couldn't be at the stars; such a desperado was neither astrologer nor astronomer.

From *A Terribly Strange Bed*, by Wilkie Collins.

F Language and style

10   Give modern synonyms for the words in bold in Passage **B**. The first one has been done for you as an example.

    a preternaturally *inexplicably/abnormally* _____

    b perseveringly _____

    c convulsively _____

    d vexation _____

    e diverting _____

    f forebodings _____

    g unwholesome _____

    h adorned _____

    i ruffian _____

11   List, with examples, the ways in which suspense and tension have been created in Passage **B**. Consider the effect of the setting, the atmosphere and the language.

_____

_____

_____

_____

_____

_____

_____

_____

_____

_____

_____

_____

_____

G Comprehension and summary

12   Complete the sentences using ideas from Passage **B**. Remember to put in the necessary commas.

    a After having _____

_____

    b Before _____

_____

c Not only _____

_____

d Even though _____

_____

e In spite of _____

_____

H Directed writing

13 The traveller has won a lot of money in a casino before a stranger persuades him to stay in this particular hotel, which turns out to be run by a gang of criminals. He just manages to roll off and escape when the top of the four-poster bed moves down to crush him. Write his report for the police the following day, using details from the passage, inference, and facts of your own.

I Composition

Descriptive writing

a Describe a room that has a strange or frightening atmosphere.
- Decide on a structure: e.g. looking around you 360 degrees; wall by wall; floor to ceiling; object by object in logical order, i.e. large and striking first to smaller and less noticeable last. What is your position in the room?
- Which objects and aspects of the room will be described in detail?
- How many senses can you include, and what imagery?

b Describe the experience of waking up in a place you don't recognise.
- Describe what you see, hear, smell and touch on waking up.
- Describe what you are thinking and how you are feeling about your baffling situation.
- Describe what you discover about the place when you get up and move around.

Narrative writing

c Write a story set at night in which an enemy attack takes place.
- What is the setting and who is the enemy?
- Who are the characters involved?
- Narrate the sequence of events of the attack and its outcome.

d Write a story that begins 'She knew that she was not going to get any sleep that night'.
- Set the scene: time, place, season, weather.
- Who is the persona, why is she there, and how does she know?
- What happens next?

Unit 11: Sub-zero

A Reading

1   Read the article below.

Passage A: Snow comfort

I'm standing on what feels like two fixed skis, holding on to what looks like the back of a wooden chair, yelling with what I hope sounds like <u>authority</u>. I am **bowling along** a snowy path at about 18 kilometres per hour under the <u>impetus</u> of a team of six husky dogs. Scandinavia offers husky sledging for tourists. **Blessed with** plentiful snow, but **cursed with** a largely flat terrain, the Scandinavian countries market their own winter sports.

The <u>masterstroke</u>, however, was the creation of IceHotel. Now a world-famous attraction, it is built **from scratch** every year on the banks of the Torne River, deep in Swedish Lapland and firmly within the Arctic Circle, where the temperature can <u>plunge</u> as low as −50 °C, and where for days on end in winter the sun does not rise at all. Initially built in 1991 it was the first, and is still the largest, frozen <u>institution</u>. Everything that looks like glass is actually made of ice: the beds, the chandeliers, the glasses for cold drinks. At IceHotel guests stamp about in boots, mittens and snow suits, all provided by the hotel. Your ice bed comes with reindeer skins plus a cosy sleeping bag. Even so, most guests only stay one night before **heading for** warmer accommodation, Santa's secret underground grotto, or the Northern Lights.

In the daytime you can take your pick of the list of Nordic snow sports, chief of which is husky sledging. More than 150 dogs are kept in a giant kennel opposite the hotel. They pull **upward of** 10 000 IceHotel guests during the winter season. The dogs have to be fit but the guests don't; most people are happy not to drive but to just sit in the sledge and be driven. For the more traditional, there is cross-country skiing, and for the more adventurous, lassoing reindeer is one of the options. Going to a wilderness cabin in a snowmobile and staying the night is an opportunity most guests prefer to **pass on**. The <u>highlight</u> of this experience is the sauna, so hot that one has to take <u>periodic</u> tumbles in the snow outside.

For a holiday with a difference, it's **hard to beat,** and makes a good topic of conversation when you get back home. Not many people have stayed in a giant luxury igloo or been <u>hurtled</u> across a snowy landscape by a pack of wolf-dogs. I have been invited out much more often since I had these tales to tell!

B Language and style

2 Find synonyms for the following idiomatic phrases as used in Passage A. The first one has been done for you as an example.

a bowling along *moving fast*

b blessed with _____

c cursed with _____

d from scratch _____

e heading for _____

f upward of _____

g pass on _____

h hard to beat _____

3 Use the underlined words in Passage A in sentences of your own to show their meaning.

a authority _____

b impetus _____

c masterstroke _____

d plunge _____

e institution _____

f highlight _____

g periodic _____

h hurtled _____

C Comprehension and summary

4 Write an advertisement for IceHotel in Lapland.

_____

_____

_____

_____

_____

_____

_____

_____

_____

D Directed writing

5 Write a letter or email to a friend back home describing your stay in IceHotel.

E Reading

6 Read the journal entries below.

Passage B: On thinning ice

Sam Branson, son of the millionaire entrepreneur and owner of the Virgin group, Sir Richard Branson, is on an epic 1200 mile expedition across the Arctic to witness how climate change is affecting one of the world's most remote places. Here are some extracts from his diary of the journey.

23rd April

I've just spent my first night sleeping in a tent in the Arctic. I woke up at 7:00 a.m. and the wind was howling. Snow had covered the base of the tent and the sun was up and full. It wasn't too cold inside the tent but once out of your sleeping bag you need to put your clothes on quickly.

I had felt no sense of isolation sleeping out on the ice and only little frissons of fear when there were strange sounds outside – your thoughts turn to polar bears and wolves. I wasn't lonely – I loved it. I felt at peace.

24th April

I woke up this morning from a deep sleep. By night-time I feel so exhausted because we're working non-stop but also because the cold takes it out of you. After a long meeting about the expedition, we organised our food rations for the weeks ahead.

Our breakfast consists of granola and oats. Lunch is carbohydrate bars, soup and nuts, and dinner is pasta or rice. Somehow, we have to eat a block of butter a day to keep our energy levels up.

This afternoon Simon and I went to build an igloo. Simon is great. He's one of the three Inuit hunters with our party and he's got a true sense of humour. He knows the environment well and I feel safer having him around. He killed his first polar bear when he was six.

28th April

We woke up this morning and left the mountainous valley where we had camped overnight. It was a clear morning with a chill in the air but by 11.00 a.m. the temperature was perfect. We now have a six-day trek across the land in front of us and I think it's going to get much trickier.

1st May

The past two weeks have been uncharacteristically warm and sunny for this time of year, but the most dangerous thing is the intensity of the UV radiation, especially coupled with the highly reflective nature of the snow. Exposure of skin and eyes can be a problem so wearing sunglasses is essential.

At around 4:00 p.m. we came to the frozen MacDonald River. The deep, soft snow in the shaded river gorge made travelling arduous but worse was to come. Following the other members of the group, we realised that the ice was very weak. Every now and again we heard loud cracking noises underneath us. It was stomach-churning. The sharp snap sends chills up your body and you hope the crack doesn't catch up with your feet. You want to turn around and look but you can't stop – you have to move forward. If you fall in, you're pretty much finished. The water is so cold – minus 40 °C – that you can freeze in seconds.

93

7th May

Last night, I woke to the sounds of the dogs barking. Through the commotion I heard someone shout: 'Polar bear!' A hundred thoughts raced through my mind. How close was it? Was someone hurt? I looked at my watch – it was 2:30 a.m. I jumped out of my sleeping bag. When I emerged I saw the bear was about 15 metres away and surrounded by mist, making it seem somewhat mysterious. The low-lying sun coated its fur in a yellowish light and its breath condensed in the cold air.

The bear stared us down, then started to run towards us. Someone fired a cracker shell into the air. These sound like firework bangers and are very good for scaring away animals. The shells are also powerful enough to kill a person.

The bear was a little startled and stopped its charge but didn't retreat. It looked magnificent – it was the size of a truck but as agile as a cat. We could see it smelling the air and checking us out as it walked closer. When it got to about 7 metres away one of the Inuit guys shot another cracker shell in the air. There are two cracker shells in the gun – the rest is live ammo.

After this second shot was fired the bear was startled but then charged forward again with real purpose. It looked hungry. It was a large male and they don't scare easily. The bear was ready to attack and was showing all the signs of dangerous behaviour. Some more shots were fired. The bear stopped and moved back a little, still eying up his targets.

The Inuit are polar-bear hunters by culture and one of them now ran towards the bear firing live shots just past it. The bear ran away and gradually melted into the snow around him. Wow, what a feeling! Scared, exhilarated, awed. What an impressive creature! It moved with such grace and power. However harmless it seemed, it was a stealth bomber – sleek and beautiful but deadly.

8th May

Global warming has consequences for animals at all levels of the Arctic food chain. Population decline anywhere along the chain has a bigger impact in the Arctic than it might in a warmer climate where there are more animals to fill each niche. The increase in non-native species migrating north is also a concern in the warming Arctic. These species compete with native species for limited resources in an already fragile food web, creating more stress on the eco-system as a whole.

10th May

Now we have almost reached the end of our journey, I reflected that the battle for the planet as we know it is being played out on the sea ice.

Extra energy being produced around the world is being absorbed into the ocean, increasing sea temperatures and melting the Arctic ice. It means the ice season, which is so important to the Inuit for hunting and travelling, is diminishing – down from eight months to six months. As the Inuit say: 'Yes, shorter winter seasons mean that we'll have to adapt and make do. Our question to you is, 'Can your culture adapt when these changes occur?'

From Sam Branson's *Arctic Diary: Surviving on thin ice*, 2007, Virgin Books, Random House

F Language and style

7 Join sentences together to make one complex sentence for each of the three paragraphs in the journal entry for 24th April in Passage **B.**

i _____

_____

_____

ii _____

_____

_____

iii _____

_____

_____

8 What stylistic features does Sam Branson use to convey a sense of suspense and tension in his description of the encounter with the polar bear in the 7th May extract?

_____

_____

_____

_____

_____

_____

_____

G Comprehension and summary

9 Write the list of questions an interviewer might ask Sam Branson in order to obtain the information given in the journal extracts.

_____

_____

_____

_____

_____

_____

_____

10 Rewrite the entry for 8th May in your own words.

_____

_____

_____

_____

_____

_____

_____

_____

_____

_____

11 In one sentence for each, summarise:

a Sam's pleasures in being in the Arctic. _____

_____

_____

_____

_____

_____

_____

_____

_____

b Sam's worries about the future of the Arctic. _____

_____

_____

_____

_____

_____

_____

_____

H Directed writing

12 Write a magazine article about Sam Branson's experience, based on the journal entries in Passage **B**. Explore his reasons for going on the expedition, what preparations and skills were required, what he learnt from it and the conclusions he drew from it.

_____

_____

_____

_____

_____

_____

_____

_____

_____

_____

_____

_____

_____

_____

_____

_____

_____

_____

_____

_____

_____

_____

_____

_____

_____

_____

_____

_____

13 Write a letter to Sam Branson in which you evaluate his ideas about climate change and express your own.

_____

_____

_____

_____

_____

_____

_____

_____

_____

_____

_____

_____

_____

_____

_____

_____

_____

_____

_____

_____

_____

_____

_____

_____

_____

_____

_____

_____

_____

_____

_____

_____

_____

_____

_____

_____

_____

_____

_____

_____

_____

_____

_____

_____

I Composition

Descriptive writing

a Describe a snowy landscape.

- Plan according to a chronological structure of changing perceptions as time passes, e.g. as dawn breaks or darkness falls.
- Use a range of senses and images to describe the landscape.

b Describe an experience of travelling over ice or snow, e.g. skating, skiing, snowboarding, sledding.

- Plan according to a spatial structure of movement bringing new things into view.
- Use a range of senses and images to describe the experience.

Narrative writing

c Write a story set in the Arctic.

- Think of a plot idea (TV series with an Icelandic/Scandinavian setting may help).
- Decide on a type of opening: scene setting, character introduction; shock; intrigue; _in medias res_ (middle of action or dialogue).
- Decide on a type of ending: ironic twist, cliff hanger, sad or happy resolution.

d 'They set off late at night through the fast falling snow…' Continue the story.

- Choose a country / historical period and mode of transport, e.g. medieval plus horses; present plus Alpine and skis; future nuclear winter plus sci-fi vehicles.
- Describe the surroundings, the characters and the reason for travel.
- What happens on the journey?

Unit 12: Seeing double

A Reading

1 Read the report below.

Passage A: Partners for life

The twins whom I interviewed described their relationship with their sister or brother as the most intimate relationship in their lives. While intuitive knowing or psychic awareness is something we all possess, this experience is heightened when you are a twin. Even when twins are out of touch and out of verbal contact for a while, one twin can sense it's time to touch in because something important is happening in the other's life. The level of **intimacy** and connection commonly experienced between twins provides a model of closeness hard to replicate in other relationships.

Anne and Liz Keliher, 37, are identical twins, born just three minutes apart. "I probably feel less alone in the world because I am a twin," *reflects* Anne. "I have more of a sense of home. I have a sense there will always be someone who understands me – how I feel, how I think and who even shares my thoughts and feelings. As long as Liz is here, celebrating special occasions, talking to someone who will really listen and care about me... I am guaranteed to have that in my life."

"On the other hand, on your birthday it's about you and someone else," *notes* Liz, "so, you've never had the experience of it being all about you."

Anne and Liz have worked hard to define who they are both as individuals and in relationship to their twin. "Even though we come from the same genetic code, as soon as we were born, we started to live separate experiences," comments Anne. "There was nature and nurture. We felt the **impact** of how we were treated by family, in classrooms. ... The different experiences changed me both emotionally and physically. And while we look a lot alike, even physically there are many differences. My face is longer and narrower. I weigh less. We have different smiles and different colour eyes. Some people think we look like regular sisters although a lot of people think we look like twins."

Liz *acknowledges*, "Defining my identity and working on individuality have taken a lot of my energy. It has been a big focus for me. Being a twin was a nice base to have. I don't think I have wrestled with my twinship being a source of identity confusion as much as Anne. The only times I've wrestled with it are when people have negative perceptions."

"Being a twin has been the impetus to explore my identity," says Anne. "I'm a very reflective person. There's so much more to explore, to reflect on because I'm a twin. The world puts the question to me – how are you different from your sister if you look so much alike? I take that cue from the world and reflect on it."

Anne and Liz spoke also of how being a twin can simultaneously make you feel more connected and more alone. "You expect an **affinity** with people that isn't achievable, at least not easily," *comments* Liz. "So, I've experienced a sense of aloneness more deeply and a sense of connection more deeply."

"There is a sense of separateness from other people who don't understand or fear being a twin because it is different," acknowledges Anne. "That's where the sense of greater aloneness comes from."

Liz speaks of her experience. "I think you're always looking for a bond with people that approaches your understanding with your twin with romantic relationships. I seek an intensity that most people feel is unattainable. My boyfriend thinks I have unrealistic expectations of how much he can understand me, because I have an understanding with Anne I don't have to work for completely."

She *continues*, "There are certain unique things a romantic partnership could encompass that ours can't. In terms of shared experience, it is hard to compete with that. With Anne, the foundation is a given. There is an understanding of where the other person is coming from because you were there for all of it – the whole childhood thing. That makes communication easier."

Anne and Liz have a younger sister Meg, who may have suffered in the shadows of the twins. "The happiness when shared with my twin is deeper, but the suffering is easier to feel as well. It's easier to feel my twin's suffering than my other sister's," *describes* Anne. "The biggest **polarisation** in our family was bad cop/good cop," adds Liz. "We were the good ones. Our sister Meg was the bad one. We got good grades. Meg didn't. Our parents looked at us as an **entity**. Liz was the extroverted side. Anne was the introverted side. You need both sides for the entity to be whole." As a single-born sibling, things were dramatically different for Meg.

Partners for Life: The Experience of Being a Twin [abridged] by Linda Marks.

101

B Language and style

2 a What do the following underlined expressions in Passage **A** mean?

psychic awareness _____

genetic code _____

nature and nurture _____

b What do the **prefixes** on the following words mean?

interviewed _____

extrovert _____

introvert _____

confusion _____

reflective _____

perception _____

encompass _____

simultaneously _____

3 Underline the spelling hot-spots in the following words and then write each word without looking at it. Check you have written it correctly.

possess   heightened   guaranteed   acknowledges   wrestled
....

4 Note the range of speech verbs italicised in Passage A. What others could have been used?

_____

5 a What is the effect of the use of direct speech in Passage **A**?

_____

_____

_____

_____

C Comprehension and summary

6 Use the following nouns, in bold in Passage **A,** in sentences of your own to illustrate their meaning.

a intimacy _____

_____

_____

_____

b impact _____

_____

_____

_____

c affinity _____

_____

_____

_____

d polarisation _____

_____

_____

_____

e entity _____

_____

_____

_____

7 Write a a summary in your own words of about 120 words of what twins experience, according to Passage A.

_____

_____

_____

_____

_____

_____

_____

_____

_____

_____

_____

_____

_____

_____

_____

_____

D Directed writing

8   **Write the transcript of an interview with Meg, the younger sibling of the twin sisters in Passage A. The questions are provided. You may infer/add extra material for the answers.**

What do you remember about your childhood?

_____

_____

_____

_____

_____

_____

What was your relationship with your sisters?

_____

_____

_____

_____

_____

_____

_____

How did your parents treat you, compared to the way they treated your sisters?

_____

_____

_____

_____

_____

_____

_____

How do you feel about your sisters now?

_____

_____

_____

_____

_____

_____

E Reading

9   Read the newspaper article below.

Passage B: Twin Town

A team of experts who visited the remote tropical Indian village of Kodinhi, in the Malappuram district of the southern state of Kerala, have been left baffled by the extraordinary phenomenon of six times as many twins being born there than **accords** with the global average. The mysterious village, popularly known as Twin Town, has produced 220 sets of twins in a population of just 2000 people. In *practice*, that means approximately 10% of the town's population are a twin. For every 1000 births in Kodinhi, 45 are twins, whereas in the rest of India it is 4 in 1000. In 2008, out of 300 healthy deliveries, 15 were pairs of twins. In the last five years alone up to 60 pairs of twins have been born – with the rate of twins increasing year-on-year. The majority of twins are identical of the same sex. Whether the women marry within the village or with men from other villages is **immaterial**.

The local doctor, 40-year-old Dr Krishnan Sribiju, has been studying the medical marvel of Kodinhi for the past five years. He believes the real number of twins to be far higher than the 220 sets officially registered. 'In my medical opinion there are around 300 to 350 twins within the village boundaries of Kodinhi,' he said. 'What is fascinating is the increasing numbers of twins with each passing year, so much so that in the past ten years the number of twins in Kodinhi has doubled.'

According to villagers, the twin phenomenon only started to *occur* three generations ago, in 1949. There are now twins of every age in the community. The local school has 30–40 sets of twins at any one time. With the majority of twins in Kodinhi being of the identical kind and the fact that a large percentage are under the age of twenty, the opportunities to *practise* mischief at school and beyond is enormous.

Dr Sribiju is excited by the possible scientific implications of the unique miracle of the village.

'Without access to detailed biochemical analysis equipment I cannot say for certain what the reason for the twinning is, but I feel that it is something to do with what the villagers eat and drink.' It is known that Igbo-Ora in Nigeria has the highest rate of twin births in the world, and one theory attributes this fact to the eating of tropical yams. If diet is the explanation, then he believes that whatever is causing this exceptional level of twinning may be used to provide help for infertile couples.

Categorising the twin phenomenon as a naturally *occurring* **anomaly**, Dr Sribiju has ruled out genetic factors as the cause due to the localised nature of the village. He also dismisses any suggestion that the unusual level of twins could be caused by an unknown pollutant, pointing to the high number of healthy twins born without any deformities. 'The number of twins per thousand here is around 45 per 1000 births. This is an extraordinary **concentration** when you consider that Indian, and by that I mean Asian, people on the sub-continent have the lowest acknowledged incidences of twinning in the world at around four per thousand.'

There is no IVF treatment available, because of the **prohibitive** cost, so the reason for the rise of rates of twins being born in the west does not affect India. Also, twins are born usually to older, more mature women. In Kodinhi that is not the case because women marry much younger, between 18 and 20 years old, and they start their families soon afterwards. Another factor that bucks the trend is that twins occur in women who are generally over 5 ft 3 inches (160.02 cm) in height. The average height of women in Kodinhi is around 5 ft (152.40 cm).'

Dr Sribiju is currently trying to assemble the research support he needs to delve deeper into the reasons for the existence of the twin town of Kodinh. He believes it is essential that there should be an in-depth study of the genetic, biological and climatic factors in order to determine the cause of this puzzling case of multiple births.

F Language and style

10 **a** Note that *practise* and *practice* both occur in Passage **B**. Study the way the words have been used, then consider the following similar pairs: *advise* and *advice, license* and *licence, prophesy* and *prophecy*. Complete the rule below.

There is a small group of usually two-syllabled words which have a slightly different spelling

for the _____ form and the _____ form. We spell the word with

an s when we are referring to the _____ , but with a c when we are using the

_____.

b Note the spelling in Passage **B** of *occur* and *occurring*. Then consider the spelling of *controlled, transferred* and *transmitted*. These verbs double the final consonant before adding -*ed* or -*ing*. List other two-syllable verbs ending in *l, r* or *t*, with the stress on the second syllable, which follow the same rule.

_____

_____

_____

_____

_____

_____

_____

_____

_____

_____

_____

c Choose the correct spelling in the following pairs by circling the word.

prefered	preferred	referal	referral
offering	offerring	deterent	deterrent
transference	transferrence	instals	installs
reference	referrence	benefited	benefitted

11 **Give synonyms for the following words in bold in Passage B.**

a accords _____

b immaterial _____

c anomaly _____

d concentration _____

e prohibitive _____

G Comprehension and summary

12　**a**　List all the facts relating to the birth of twins in Passage **B**.

six times higher than global average

_____

_____

_____

_____

_____

_____

_____

_____

b　List all the theories relating to the birth of twins in Passage **B**.

diet may be the cause

_____

_____

_____

_____

_____

_____

_____

_____

_____

_____

13　**Fill in the gaps to complete the summary of Passage B. Use your own words. The first one has been done for you as an example.**

Experts have been unable to find a (1) _solution_____ to the mystery of what has been
(2) _____ the Twin Town of India, where a (3)_____ number of twin births
has become a (4)_____ phenomenon, and one which is inexplicable. The local doctor
is (5)_____ that there should be research done to (6)_____ the cause,
so that the findings can be applied to fertility treatments. None of the theories which have been
(7)_____ are relevant to this case so far, but the doctor believes that diet may prove to
be a (8)_____ factor. In the meantime, the experts continue to be (9)_____
and the twins continue to enjoy being able to (10)_____ their teachers and neighbours.

H Directed writing

14   Write a letter from Dr Sribirju to an international medical magazine, explaining what is happening in Kodhini and why funding for research should be provided.

_____

_____

_____

_____

_____

_____

_____

_____

_____

_____

_____

_____

_____

_____

_____

_____

_____

_____

_____

_____

_____

_____

_____

_____

_____

_____

_____

_____

_____

I Composition

Descriptive writing

a Describe the moment when long separated family members reunite.

- Who are the members who have not seen each other for many years?
- What happened to cause their separation and to bring them back together?
- Who is present at the reunion, and how does everyone behave?

b Describe the real or imaginary experience of meeting your exact lookalike.

- Describe the appearance of the lookalike, and explain where and when this meeting took place.
- Who was present and how did they react?
- What did it make you think and feel?

Narrative writing

c 'The mysterious village'. Write a story with this title.

- Decide on a historical or imaginary period (past, present or future) and describe the setting.
- Describe the inhabitants of the village, their way of life, and what the mystery is.
- Narrate a particular event that leads to a dramatic ending.

d Write a story involving identical twins.

- Introduce the main characters: name, age, appearance, background.
- Describe the relationship of the twins and their customary behaviour.
- Narrate a particular event that leads to a dramatic ending.

Grammar and punctuation reference

Grammar

Grammar prefixes (Units 1, 2, 3, 4, 6, 7, 12)

- English words often have prefixes. Knowing what the different prefixes are will help you work out the meaning of a word. The table below shows common prefixes, what they mean and examples of words in which they appear.

Prefix	Meaning	Example
ante-	before	antenatal
anti-	against	antifreeze
con-	together	conjoined
de-	opposite	defrost
dis-	not, opposite of	disagree
en-, em-	cause to	encode, embrace
ex-	out	exit
fore-	before	forecast
hyper-	above	hyperactive
hypo-	below	Hypothermia
in-	in	Include
in-, im-, il-, ir-	not	injustice, impossible, illogical, irreparable
inter-	between	interact
intra-	within	intravenous
mid-	middle	midway
mis-	wrongly	Misfire
non-	not	nonsense
over-	over	overlook
post-	after	postgraduate
pre-	before	Prefix
pro-	towards, for	progress
re-	again	Return
semi-	half	semicircle
sub-	under, below	submarine
super-	above	superstar
syn-	together	synthesise
trans-	across	transport
un-	not	unfriendly
under	under	underground

- The most common can be learnt in pairs of opposite meaning, e.g. *super* (above) / *sub* (below); *in* (in) / *ex* (out); *pre* (before) / *post* (after); *pro* (for, towards) / *anti* (against).
- Prefixes come from both Greek and Latin, which means there are often two prefixes with the same meaning, e.g. *con* and *syn* (together).
- Some are very similar and easily confused, e.g. *hyper* (above) and *hypo* (below); *inter* (between) and *intra* (within); *anti* (against) and *ante* (before).
- The negative prefixes are *mis* (e.g. mistake), *dys* (e.g. dystopia), *dis* (e.g. dissatisfied), *un* (e.g. unhygienic) and *in* (e.g. insatiable) – not to be confused with *in* meaning in.
- Prefixes can alter their final letter according to the first letter of the stem they are attached to, e.g. *syn* (with) + pathy becomes sympathy; *con* (together) + location becomes *col*location.
- Some prefixes have an actual meaning rather than simply a grammatical one (and are sometimes called root words), e.g. *astro* means star, *psy* means mind, *chrono* means time, *phil* means love.
- There is a full range of number prefixes, e.g. *mono* (Greek) and *uni* (Latin) mean one; *tetra* (Greek) and *quad* (Latin) mean four; *kilo* (Greek) and *mill* (Latin) mean a thousand.

Parts of speech (Units 1, 4, 5, 8)

- 'Part of speech' is the term used to indicate the role a word plays in a sentence.
- The main ones are noun, verb, adjective and adverb
  - i **nouns** are objects (things that can be seen, touched, smelled etc.), e.g. roof, book, perfume or concepts (things that cannot be seen, touched, smelled, etc.), e.g. idea, plan, love. The test of a noun is whether it is possible to put *'the'*, *'an'* or *'a'* in front of it: *'the roof is leaking'*, *'she had an idea'*, *'they had a plan'*.
  - ii **Verbs** are actions or processes. They can be physical or mental, e.g. dig, collapse, think, anticipate. The test of a verb is whether it is possible to make it an infinitive (*where the word isn't in the past, present or future tense*) by putting 'to' in front of it: *'to dig a hole'*, *'to anticipate good news'*.
  - iii **adjectives** describe nouns, e.g. blue, cosy, sharp, huge. Sometimes they are the present or past participle of the verb, e.g. *flowing* river, *broken* bottle. Sometimes they are the same as the noun form, e.g. *secret* message, *square* table. A test of an adjective is whether it can go immediately before a noun: *'the cosy chair'*.
  - iv **adverbs** explain how a verb is performed, e.g. *slowly, terrifyingly, badly, cheerfully*. With rare exceptions (e.g. *hard, fast*) they are made by adding 'ly' to an adjective. If the adjective ends in 'l' the adverb will end in 'lly', e.g. *faithful – faithfully*. Not all words ending in 'ly' are adverbs though; many adjectives *also* end in 'ly', e.g. *costly, deadly, chilly*. A test of an adverb is whether it can go immediately after a verb, e.g. *'the boys sat quietly'*.
- **Prepositions** are words which indicate the relative position or movement of two things, e.g. the cat is *under* the table; the pen fell *behind* the bookcase; the children are going *to* the cinema; the picture is *on* the wall. They can also be used in common phrases, e.g. to think about; out of the question; of course ; by accident.

Passive voice (Unit 1)

- The usual form of the verb is called the 'active' form. In an active sentence the <u>subject</u> performs the *verb*, e.g. <u>they</u> *noticed* the mistake; <u>we</u> *will do* it tomorrow; the <u>dog</u> *bit* the man. The 'passive voice' is made by placing the verb '<u>to be</u>' (am, is, are, were, being, been, be, etc.) in its active form before the ***past participle form of the second verb***, e.g. the mistake <u>was</u> **noticed**; it <u>will be</u> **done** tomorrow; the man <u>was</u> **bitten** by the dog
- If the subject needs to be mentioned after a passive verb, then it follows the preposition *by*, as in the last example.

- Passive verb forms are mainly used in non-fiction, informative, discursive and scientific writing, e.g. text books, political texts, instruction manuals. They are also used when speaking. They tend to make sentences more tactful, impersonal, formal or objective and give authority to the text and the writer/speaker. The emphasis in the sentence is on the object or event and not on the human doing it. The human is often not mentioned at all: *the mistake was noticed; it will be done tomorrow; Germany was beaten in the final match; the results of the research were published in an international journal.*

Quantifiers (Unit 1)

Quantifiers are used before nouns to indicate the amount or quantity of something.

- Positive quantifiers are *much* for uncountable nouns (e.g. *much* trouble) and *many* for countable nouns (e.g. *many* cakes). Their comparative (used when comparing) and superlative (used when showing the *highest*, the *biggest* or the *best*) forms are the same, i.e. *more* and the *most* (e.g. *more* trouble, the *most* money).

- The negative quantifier for uncountable nouns is *little* (e.g. *little* food). For countable nouns it is *few* (e.g. *few* children). Their comparative forms are *less* and *fewer* (e.g. *less/fewer* food). Their superlative forms are the *least* and the *fewest* (e.g. the *fewest* children).

- *A few* and *a little* are used positively to mean *some*, so 'few students turned up' is stressing their absence, whereas 'a *few* students turned up' stresses their presence.

Complex sentences (Units 5, 10, 11)

- Simple sentences have only one main verb, e.g. The cat *ate* some food.
- Compound sentences have two equal main verbs, joined by 'and', 'but', 'so' or 'or', e.g. The cat *ate* some food and then it *went* to sleep; we *noticed* it but we *didn't* say anything.
- Complex sentences link *subordinate* (less important) clauses to a main clause (which could stand alone as a sentence), e.g. The cat went to sleep, *after it ate some food*.
- The *subordinate clause* could go in front of the main clause, i.e. *After it ate some food*, the cat went to sleep. It could also go in the middle of the main clause, i.e. The cat, *after it ate some food,* went to sleep. The order can change where the emphasis falls in the sentence.
- Connectives (linking words,) used at the beginning of the subordinate clause, can be used to form a complex sentence. There are many connectives which can be used, e.g. before, after, because, whenever, although. Some are similar in meaning, e.g. for and since. Some are more than one word, e.g. even though.
- A comma is used to show the 'join' between the main clause and the subordinate clause.
- A sentence can have several subordinate clauses.
- Writing in complex sentences, using a range of connectives, is the basic form of advanced written communication and formal speech.

Defining and non-defining relative clauses (Unit 7)

- Relative clauses are clauses that begin with *who, that, which, whose, where or when*.
- Non-defining relative clauses can be added to a main clause by the use of who (for a person) or which (for a non-person). They are called non-defining because they are not part of the definition of the person or object noun. They are used to give additional information. Also, the main clause can stand alone without the *additional information*, e.g. They greeted the postman, *who was delivering letters*; The essay, *which had mistakes in,* had to be done again; The athletes, *who failed the drugs test*, were disqualified.

- Unlike non-defining relative clauses, defining relative clauses don't use commas. For example, The athletes who failed the drugs text were disqualified. (This implies that there were also other athletes who did not fail the test, and so were not disquaified.)

Past tenses (Unit 7)

There are six main ways to talk about the past in English:

i **present perfect** – formed with the <u>present tense</u> of have (has) plus the *past participle of the verb*. It is used for an action completed at an unspecified time in the past, e.g. She <u>has</u> *written* the book.

ii **present perfect continuous** – formed with the <u>'present perfect' tense</u> of have (has) plus the *present participle* of the verb. It is used for an action begun in the past but not yet completed, e.g. She <u>has</u> <u>been</u> *writing* the book.

iii **past simple** – formed with the *past form of the verb*. It is used for a completed and time-specific action, e.g. She *wrote* the book last year.

iv **past continuous** – formed with was/were plus the present participle. It is used when an action that is <u>already occurring</u> is interrupted by another action, e.g. <u>She was writing the book</u> *when she went to Australia.*

v **past perfect** – formed with the <u>past tense of have</u> (had) plus the *past participle of the verb*. It is used when an action occurred before another action in the past, e.g. <u>She had</u> *written* the book before she went to Australia.

vi **past perfect continuous** – formed with the <u>'past perfect' of have (had)</u> plus the *present participle*. It is used to show that an action stopped when another action interrupted it, e.g. She <u>had been</u> *writing* the book before she went to Australia.

Connectives (linking words) (Unit 8)

- Linking words (discourse markers/paragraph links) are adverbial words or phrases used at the beginning of a paragraph or sentence to show the direction of an argument or discussion. Without them, the reader will find it more difficult to follow the writer's thought process, and the writing will be less cohesive.

- Two categories are:

    i **extending** (i.e. continuing an argument/ discussion in the same direction) e.g. Furthermore, In addition, Moreover, Similarly

    ii **contrasting** (i.e. turning against the previous point of view), e.g. Nonetheless, Nevertheless, On the other hand, However, Yet, Conversely

- A comma is needed after a linking word or phrase.

Conditional sentences (Unit 10)

Conditional sentences are sentences which contain 'if' or 'unless'. There are four types of conditional sentence.

i <u>'If' or 'unless' followed by the present simple tense</u> in the secondary (subordinate) clause, and *will + verb infinitive (without 'to')* in the main clause, e.g. <u>If you keep doing</u> that, *you will* fall over; <u>unless you</u> <u>leave</u> early, *you will* get stuck in traffic. This type is for probable future outcomes.

ii <u>'If' or 'unless' followed by the past simple tense</u> in the secondary clause, and *would + verb infinitive (without 'to')* in the main clause. e.g. <u>If we continued</u> along the path, we *would arrive* at the car park; <u>Unless we ran out</u> of money, *we would stay* for two weeks.

This type is for possible outcomes and hypothetical situations.

iii <u>If/unless in the secondary clause</u> followed by *the past perfect tense*, and 'would have' + *verb with past participle* in the main clause, e.g. <u>If they had studied</u> harder, they *would have passed* their exams. This type is for impossible outcomes (i.e. hypothetical situations).

iv The present simple tense in both clauses, e.g. If <u>you turn</u> in circles very fast, <u>you become</u> dizzy; Unless <u>you stir</u> a sauce, it <u>has lumps</u> in it. This type is for facts / permanent truths, which are sometimes called 'zero conditionals' because no conditions are required.

- The order of the clauses can be reversed, e.g. They would have passed their exams, if they had studied harder.
- There is usually a comma between the two clauses, especially when the secondary clause comes first.

Punctuation

Parentheses (Unit 2)
A parenthesis is a word, phrase, clause, comment or explanation inserted into a sentence. If you remove the parenthesis from the sentence it should still be grammatically complete. Parenthesis are formed by pairs of commas, dashes or brackets.

- The type of punctuation used around parenthesis depends on how closely connected the extra (**parenthetical**) information is to the content of the main sentence. Commas imply the closest connection, and brackets suggest the least, because they have the strongest visual impact of separation. e.g. 'Two minutes later, Mo's car (music blaring from the open windows) sped past.'
- The punctuation marks work as a pair so it is important not to forget the closing one.
- The test of whether you have put your two marks in the right place is to read the sentence without the material contained between them, to see if it makes sense.
- For variety, a range of all three types may be used in the same text, and one sentence may contain more than one parenthesis.

Dashes and hyphens (Units 3, 7, 9)
Dashes and hyphens look similar but have very different functions.

- Dashes are twice as wide as hyphens (in handwriting). They have a space either side and are used singly (only once) to add on a clarification or an apparently spontaneous afterthought, e.g. I wasn't very happy about the situation – in fact I was furious; No one wanted to go – least of all him.
- Dashes are more likely to be found in less formal writing, where first thoughts are often modified to make them sound unplanned or colloquial.
- Dashes are also used in pairs to form a parenthesis around extra explanatory material.
- Hyphens do not have spaces before or after. They are used to join two or more words together in a compound, to show that the meaning is inter-dependent, e.g. mother-in-law, old-fashioned, five-year-old, red-faced, backward-looking.
- Hyphens are used in compound numbers to separate the tens and the units from twenty-one to ninety-nine.
- Hyphens are more likely to be found in formal writing, where complex or technical vocabulary is used. They are also used in poetry and descriptive writing where density of meaning, specific and multiple details, and condensed similes are used to create powerful effects. Colour adjectives, for

example, are likely to be compounds, as olive-green or slate-grey is more precise than just green or grey. They also evoke an image.

- Hyphens are sometimes used between a <u>prefix</u> and the *stem* of a word, especially if without the hyphen the word would be very long, e.g. <u>multi</u>-*faceted*, <u>extra</u>-*terrestrial*, or cause confusion, e.g. no-one, co-operate, mis-spelling. But this is often a matter of personal style, and the general tendency is to not use hyphens where they are optional.

Apostrophes (Units 4, 9)
We use apostrophes either when we wish to **signal omission** of letters (e.g. can't,) or when we wish to **show possession** (e.g. one week's time, the dog's tail).

- An apostrophe after the final s of a word, unless it is a name, indicates that the possessor is plural (e.g. the girls' books).

- If the possessor's name ends in an 's', the apostrophe will still go after the name, but it is optional not to add another 's', e.g. Atticus' spectacles instead of Atticus's spectacles.

- If the possessor has an irregular (unusual) plural form, e.g. child – children, the plural possession is shown by the apostrophe going immediately after the plural form, and then an 's' is added, e.g. the children's toys, the people's choice.

- We use an apostrophe in **it's** if the meaning is **it is** or **it has**, e.g. it's raining; it's been lost, whereas **its** without an apostrophe is used to **show possession**, e.g. the dog wagged its tail; they didn't like its appearance.

- It is not necessary to put an apostrophe in the plural of an acronym or number, e.g. the 1960s, IGCSEs.

Semi-colons (Units 4, 7, 9)
- Semi-colons have a similar function to full stops. They are used between two sentences (often short) that are closely connected in meaning, e.g. the thunder rumbled; the wind started to blow.

- A semi-colon can replace a connective to make more concise or dramatic expression, e.g. I came; I saw; I conquered.

- Semi-colons can also be used to separate items in a list. This is usually done when the items are longer than one word or where commas might be confusing. The list should be introduced by a colon, e.g. They had to pack a lot of picnic food: cheese and tomato sandwiches; various types of crisps; chocolate, ginger and oatmeal biscuits; apples and bananas.

Direct speech / dialogue punctuation (Units 4, 6, 9)
- Inverted commas (speech marks) are used to indicate words actually spoken (or thought). They are placed at the beginning and end of direct speech. If the sentence has already begun, the speech is introduced with a comma, e.g. The teacher said, "I have some good news for you."

- In handwriting, double inverted commas are used. A quotation or a title within speech can be indicated by single inverted commas, e.g. She explained, "The headteacher said 'Why not?' when I asked if we could have the rest of the day off."; He said, "The name of our next reading book is 'Treasure Island'."

- Within speech, most of the same punctuation rules apply as for normal writing. If there is no continuation of the sentence after the end of the speech there needs to be a full stop at the end of a sentence, e.g. He said, "No". If there is a continuation, then in place of the full stop we use a comma, question mark or exclamation mark, e.g. "No," he said; "No!" he exclaimed; "No?" he queried.

- The word after the end of speech always begins with a lower-case letter rather than a capital, even after a question or exclamation mark. This is because it is continuing the sentence. e.g. "No," he said; "No!" he exclaimed; "No?" he queried.
- If a sentence in speech is interrupted and then continued, there is a comma before the break and again before the re-opening of the inverted commas. The continuation will begin with a small letter, not a capital because the sentence is also continuing, e.g. "I don't believe," she said imperiously, "a single word of it."
- If the speech is part of a dialogue, start a new line for the next speaker.
- If the speech is so long that it continues beyond the end of the paragraph, as in a monologue, open inverted commas again at the start of the new paragraph. This is to remind the reader that it is still direct speech. However, do not use closing inverted commas at the end of the previous paragraph.

Commas (Units 5, 7, 9)

Commas have five main functions. In all its functions, a sentence should still be complete if the commas are removed. They are not interchangeable with full-stops, unlike semi-colons.

a to separate clauses, e.g. They were determined to go, whatever the weather.

b to create a phrase in apposition (a phrase placed next to another to help describe or define it), e.g. They, the four teams, were determined to go.

c to create a parenthesis with two commas, e.g. They were determined, despite the weather, to go.

d to separate items in a list, e.g. One had to consider the words, the thoughts, the actions, and the feelings; the young, enthusiastic, excited, gifted performers .

e after an initial adverb / linking phrase e.g. Unfortunately, they were never seen again; On the contrary, it was a highly successful expedition.

Acknowledgements

The authors and publishers acknowledge the following sources of copyright material and are grateful for the permissions granted. While every effort has been made, it has not always been possible to identify the sources of all the material used, or to trace all copyright holders. If any omissions are brought to our notice, we will be happy to include the appropriate acknowledgements on reprinting.

Unit 8 Passage B used with permission from Nextshark.com; **Unit 9** Passage A 'The Cavern Club' by Mat Rudd © The Times/NI Syndication; **Unit 11** Passage B From *Arctic Diary: On Thinning Ice* 2007 by Sam Branson, published by Virgin Books, Random House UK; **Unit 12** Passage A used with permission by the author, Linda Marks.

Thanks to the following for permission to reproduce images:
Cover AleksandarNakic/Getty Images; **Unit 1** photosindia/Getty Images; clicksbyabrar/Getty Images; **Unit 2** Thomas Niedermueller/Getty Images; Fotofeeling/Getty Images; Per-Anders Pettersson/Getty Images; **Unit 3** Education Images/UIG via Getty Images; David De Lossy/Getty Images; **Unit 4** kevinjeon00/Getty Images; **Unit 5** Kim Schandorff/Getty Images; HomoCosmicos/Getty Images; **Unit 6** JRabski/Getty Images; Azam Husain/Barcroft Images / Barcroft Media via Getty Images; **Unit 7** PHAS/UIG via Getty Images; Jonathan Howison / EyeEm/Getty Images; **Unit 8** Amar Deep/Pacific Press/LightRocket via Getty Images; Keow Wee Loong / Barcroft Images / Barcroft Media via Getty Images; **Unit 9** Loic Lagarde / Getty Images; VALERY HACHE/AFP/Getty Images; **Unit 10** In Pictures Ltd./Corbis via Getty Images; **Unit 11** craftvision/Getty Images; Andia/UIG via/Getty Images; **Unit 12** Frédéric Soltan/Corbis via Getty Images

We would like to thank the students from 10 Honour and 10 Virtue at R.E.A.L International School, Shah Alam Campus in Malaysia who generously took part in a focus group relating to the Cambridge IGCSE First Language English Language and Skills Practice Book : Ong Rou Ping, Muhammad Aliff, Jayden Samuel Adesh Koshy, Chloe Cheah Pui Yan, Marcus Yeoh Yang Yuan, Samuel Ting Soon Zhe, Marcus Chen Che Tze, Dennis Lim Yan Bin, Aminath Esha Ibrahim, Tee Ee Vent, and Amisha Rekha Christie.

117

Answers

Note: In some cases more than one correct answer is possible, or students have been asked to write their answers in their own words. Some examples are supplied: they are not prescriptive.

Unit 1

2 & 3 (Sample answers)

    a extravaganza – spectacle (noun)

    b coordinated – combined (adjective)

    c synchronised – made to happen at the same time (verb)

    d technicians – specialists (noun)

    e electric – excited (adjective)

    f incandescent – fiery (adjective)

    g iridescent – sparkling (adjective)

    h scintillating – shimmering (adjective)

    i mesmerised – entranced (adjective)

    j simultaneously – at the same time (adverb)

4 (Sample answers)

    a Use of same structure in a set of simple sentences gives the effect of a series of separate events, quickly succeeding each other, which replicates the watcher's experience.

    b The vocabulary is figurative, creating a series of metaphors describing the role of the tower and the speed of movement of the exploding fireworks. Many of the images based on nature, and these conjure the ideas of colour and beauty.

5 (Answers may include)

Para. 1: time, place and nature of the event

Para. 2: records broken

Para. 3: features of the display: countdown; flag; use of the Burj Khalifa

Para. 4: planning and statistics for the display

Para. 5: reaction and behaviour of the crowd

Para. 6: made-up quotation from an organiser and/or spectator

7   **a** *are believed; have been invented; were used; is believed; thrown; heated; are still made; were enjoyed; were achieved; is less frequently used; were added; was masterminded; set off; was produced and launched; held; are set off; was seen*

    b (Sample answer)

    Passives are predominantly used in non-fiction, informative, discursive and scientific writing or speaking, e.g. text books, political texts, instruction manuals. They tend to make expression more tactful, impersonal, formal or objective, and give authority to the text. The emphasis in the sentence falls on the object or event and not on the human agent, who is often unspecified.

8 There are **few** signs of fireworks losing popularity as a form of entertainment. Gradually, private firework shows are becoming **less** common and are being replaced by public events. This means that the injuries caused by fireworks are **fewer**, but they are still a cause of damage to property, unintended fires, maiming of children and traumatising of animals. **A few** people argue that fireworks are destructive in many senses, and that the expense and waste of natural resources cannot be justified in return for **a few** moments of pleasure, but there is **little** public debate on the subject, and unlikely to be, given that they have been around for so long.

Little (and its comparative *less* and its superlative *least*) is used before singular or non-countable nouns, like time, whereas *few* (and its comparative *fewer* and its superlative *fewest*) is used before plural and countable nouns, like hours. The indefinite article in the phrases *a little* and *a few* make the effect positive rather than negative. For example, *A few people attended* is more positive than *Few people attended*.

10 **a** the 13th

   b **(Sample answer)**
   The addition of metals to gunpowder gave fireworks a wider range of colours and made them burn with sparks.

   c Kuwait

   d **(Sample answer)**
   The speed of sound is much slower than the speed of light.

   e **(Sample answers)**
   i summon/conjure up wealth
   ii different coloured fireworks were a novelty/new invention
   iii continue to lead the way/initiate developments

11 **(Sample answers)**
   a The Chinese probably invented fireworks two millennia ago – perhaps accidentally – and are now the main producer of fireworks (despite the dangers involved in their manufacture by hand), which are used in their many festivals, including celebrations of New Year and to commemorate the invention of the firecracker.

   b Italy – a country which took a particular interest in fireworks and developed them in the 19th century – is still at the cutting edge of pyrotechnics and involved in major displays today.

   c Fireworks consist of gunpowder (saltpetre, charcoal and sulphur) mixed with various chemical compounds – depending on the colours and sounds desired – within a cardboard shell.

12 **(Sample answer)**
   Originating in the Far East in ancient times, the knowledge of gunpowder moved westwards and became known in Europe in the medieval period, when more colours were made possible by the addition of other chemicals. By the 19th century, a range of types of firework had been developed, including those with sound effects. Displays continually increase in length and spectacle, thanks to the recent use of computers to coordinate them with accompanying music. Fireworks are now used worldwide to celebrate local, national and international events.

13 **(Answers may include)**
   fireworks cause injury (blindness and maiming); waste of natural resources, such as magnesium; only last a few minutes but cost a phenomenal amount; money could be spent on something lasting and worthwhile; primitive behaviour to get excited about fire; trauma caused to wildlife and domestic animals; encourages bad feeling and one-upmanship between countries.

Unit 2

3 **(Note that alternatives are possible. The important thing is to mark the beginning and end of the parenthesis in the right place.)**

    a Wild apes have no need of language, and have not developed it, but tame ones can use it as a tool for communicating with each other.

    b Each slaughtered ape is a loss to the local community – a loss to humanity as a whole – and is a hole torn in the ecology of our planet.

    c The skills of language and counting – essential for negotiating trade – can be taught to orang-utans, who are less social primates than chimpanzees, in a matter of weeks.

    d Fifteen million years (a small gap in the broad scale of evolution) is an immense period in terms of everyday life.

    e Gorilla mothers prefer to cradle their babies on their left sides – a feature shared with humans – and there have been cases of them showing maternal behaviour to human children.

4 **a** T   **b** D   **c** D   **d** T   **e** F

5 **b** **(Sample answer)**

    Teddies were named after US President Theodore Roosevelt, who refused to shoot a cornered bear when out hunting in Mississippi in 1902. After a newspaper cartoonist had made the hunting story famous, a New York shop owner was granted permission by the President to name the bears in his shop, made by his wife, 'Teddy's Bears'.

7 **(Sample answers)**

    a Not only did the bear let children ride him, but also he played with dogs.

    b Never before had he broken his chain.

    c Neither the lady nor the cook realised what had happened.

    d No longer did the bear interfere with the bee-hives.

    e Not so much as a whimper was uttered by the bear.

8 **(Sample answers)**

    a We are told that the bear was not usually chained during the day and can infer that he did not like being chained, so lady's would expect him to break free. By calling it '*the bear*' in paragraph 5, the writer implies that it is the same one. We do not expect a wild bear to accept being hit with an umbrella. We are told that on her return the lady's bear was *looking very sorry for himself*, which suggests that he was the bear who had been hit.

    b He had been found *small and helpless* and *half-dead of hunger*. Although the bear was strong, he was gentle and friendly, and loved by dogs, children and the cook. He disliked being on a chain but was *good as gold* about it. The lady had punished him previously by making his nose bleed. It was unfair of her to threaten to deprive him of his favourite food of apples because of her own mistake.

9 **(Sample answers)**

    a A woman owned a full-grown pet bear, which she chained up when she went out. One Sunday, she met a bear in the forest on her way to her sister's house and, assuming it was her bear, she scolded and hit it for having broken its chain and followed her. The bear went away, but when the lady arrived home and found her bear still chained up, she was told by her cook that he had never left, so then she realised that she had attacked a different and wild bear.

120

b Cubs are considered appealing and vulnerable. They appear in popular children's fiction, and their image is widely used commercially. They can be tamed and kept as pets. Like children, they like sweet foods. They seem to have friendly eyes, and look cuddly. They are playful and tolerant, and get on with other animals and children.

Unit 3

2 **a** respective **b** mainly **c** part **d** vital **e** sort out

4 **(Sample answers)**
 a situation **b** supervise **c** correct **d** equivalents **e** response **f** thoroughly

5 **a** sub, ad, con, re, per, extro, co, o, a **d** re, ab, con, dis, pre
 b re, im, de, ex, pur, sup, trans **e** im, com, re, sup, ap
 c re, in, con

6 **Sentences should contain the following words with their correct meanings.**
 a proceed (go forward); precede (go before)
 b lie (no object); lay (with object)
 c affect (verb); effect (noun)
 d continuous (without breaks); continual (with breaks)
 e principal (adjective meaning main); principle (noun meaning fundamental belief)
 f whose (belonging to whom); who's (contraction of who is or who has)
 g uninterested (not interested); disinterested (not biased)

7 **a** Dashes have a space either side and are used singly to *add on an apparently spontaneous afterthought*. For example: *There were hundreds of people there – maybe thousands*.
 b Hyphens, which do not have spaces before or after, are used to *join two or more words together in a compound, to show that their meaning is dependent on each other*. For example: *mother-in-law, old-fashioned*.

8 **a** The article is aimed at readers of an in-flight or life-style magazine who want to be entertained rather than informed.
 b **(Sample answer)**
 The informal style includes: compound sentence structures; sentences beginning with *So* and *And*; the use of ellipsis for dramatic effect; missing verb *to be* (*three aircraft in Leeds and their corresponding passengers in Manchester*); questions and exclamations; single dashes; non-technical/non-specialist vocabulary; contracted verb forms (*it's, what's*);

9 **(Sample answer)**
 TopFlights charters operate out of two airports in the UK, but principally Manchester, where it is well established and the third-largest airline. It runs scheduled, high-frequency, short-distance flights. Punctuality is a high priority for the company.

10 **(Sample answer)**
 Airport managers should be calm and organised, versatile and flexible. They must be efficient across a range of skills, contexts and interactions with people. Good communication skills and a sense of humour are necessary qualities.

121

11 (Sample answer)

The job of an airport manager is to adhere to the standards of the company, to monitor processes to ensure efficient functioning, and to activate the correction of weaknesses through staff training. They must keep informed, pass on information to the company and collaborate with other airport managers for their airline. They must consider the image of the company they represent.

14 (Sample answers)

a So that if they get separated from their 'auntie', they can explain who they are and their parents can be contacted.

b In case your child needs to buy something in the airport or on the plane.

c To familiarise your child with the place so that they feels less apprehensive about the experience the next day.

d To avoid large crowds which might be overwhelming for your child.

e Because children are likely to feel more homesick and frightened at night.

f In case the flight is delayed or cancelled and your child needs to be returned to you.

g So that your child does not feel trapped amongst strangers and can go to the toilet easily.

h Your child will feel less daunted if they can see and hear other children.

17 (Sample structure)

Para. 1: Explain why you are writing and where you saw the advertisement.

Para. 2: Give your qualifications.

Para. 3: Explain how your skills fit the job description and why you would make a suitable employee.

Para. 4: Thank the recipient for their attention and say that you hope to be called for an interview.

Unit 4

2 (Sample answers)

a We use apostrophes either when we wish to signify omission of letters (for example *can't, six o'clock*) or when we wish to show possession (for example: *one week's time, the dog's tail*). An apostrophe after the final *s* of a word, unless it is a name, indicates that the possessor is plural (for example: *the girls' books*).

b We use an apostrophe in *it's* if the meaning is *it is* or *it has*, whereas *its* without an apostrophe is used to show possession (for example: *the dog wagged its tail*) (compare to *his* and *hers*).

3 Semi-colons, which are used sparingly and only for a good reason, have the same function as full stops; [semi-colon] but are used when the preceding sentence has a close connection with the following sentence. They can also be used to separate items in a list.

5 a beautiful – beautify;   b destructive – destroy;   c enduring – endure;

   d abstinence – abstain;   e pleasure – please;   f celebrities – celebrate

6 a hunter-gatherer – primitive food collectors _____

   b far-flung – extensive _____

   c no-man's-land – area between disputed boundaries _____

   d punch-ups – fights _____

   e feeding-frenzied – excitedly voracious _____

7 **(Sample answer)**

Ancient civilisations played a kind of football and exported the game to their empires. Football as we know it dates from late 12th-century in England. In 1863, after a brief lapse, it was re-established when the Football Association was set up. By the 1870s, professional teams existed, which played internationally in South America and northern Europe. FIFA evolved as an organisation, resulting in the World Cup. The modern game owes much to mass-media coverage – which began in 1927 – and consequent financial influence.

10 **a** niche – specialised

b corruption – debasement

c asymmetrical – lopsided

d proficient – accomplished

e tactical – strategic

11 Within speech, most of the same punctuation rules apply as for normal writing, so that there needs to be a **full stop** at the end of a sentence, provided that there is no continuation of the sentence after the end of the speech. If there is, then in place of the full stop we use a **comma** or, if appropriate, a question mark or exclamation mark. Even after a question or exclamation mark, the next word begins with a **lower-case** letter rather than a **capital** if it is continuing the sentence. If a sentence in speech is interrupted and then continued, there is a **comma** before the break and again before the re-opening of the inverted commas. The continuation will begin with a small letter, not a capital because the **sentence** is also continuing. There must always be a punctuation mark of some kind before the closing **inverted commas**. If a speech contains speech or quotation, then the inner speech must use the opposite kind of **inverted commas** from the outer speech, whether single or double.

12 After a single vowel, the consonant will double if the vowel sound is short (for example: *dinner* with a short vowel sound; *diner* with a long vowel sound).

13 *fore-* front, before

medi- middle

sym- alike

para- equal

en- into

14 **a** on the up – becoming more popular

b not inconsiderable – significant

c a cross between – a mixture of

d from time to time – occasionally, periodically

e give it a go – have a try at it, make an attempt

16 **Points to include:**

a Historical background: name means 'royal'; first type of tennis and other ball games played on a court; the game of kings; played on huge indoor courts; started in medieval France; taken to England in early 16th century; now has 10 000 players; played in four countries; little played for most of 20th century; has grown in popularity recently.

b Unusual features: asymmetrical court with buttress; courts differ in size; mixture of modern tennis and squash; unusual rules; suits less fit players; balls are heavy; ball comes from different directions; game of strategy more than physical skill.

Unit 5

2

Noun	Adjective	Verb	Adverb
produce, producer, product, production	**productive**	produces	**productively**
occurrence, **recurrence**	**current**	**occur, recur**	**recurringly, currently**
depth	deep	**deepen**	**deeply**
origins	**original**	**originate**	**originally**
explorers, **exploration**	**exploratory, explorative**	**explore**	**exploratively**
measure, measurement	**measurable, measured**	measured	**measurably**
sponsor, sponsorship	**sponsored**	sponsored	
conviction, convict	**convicted, convincing**	convinced, **convict**	**convincingly**
definition	**definite, finite**	**define**	definitely
extreme, extremity, extremist	extreme		**extremely**

Note: when a two-syllabled noun and a verb are spelt the same, the noun is often stressed on the first syllable and the verb on the second, e.g. pro̲duce and prod̲uce, con̲vict and convi̲ct.

3 **a** to separate clauses (e.g. *The precise source of the Amazon was only recently discovered, although the origins of most of the Earth's great rivers have been known for some time …*)

    b to create a phrase in apposition, (e.g. *the mouth of the Amazon, where it meets the sea, is so deep as well as wide …*)

    c to create a parenthesis (e.g. *A global positioning system (GPS), linked to a network of satellites, was employed …*)

    d to separate items in a list (e.g. *because of a combination of unfriendly terrain, high altitudes, cold winds …*)

    e after an initial adverb (e.g. *Famously, the Amazon river is home to many exotic …*)

4 **b** **(Sample answers)**

- The source of the Amazon, which has only recently been discovered, although explorers tried for centuries to discover it, is located 160 kilometres from the Pacific Ocean.
- Although explorers tried for centuries to discover the source of the Amazon, it has only recently been discovered, located 160 kilometres from the Pacific Ocean.
- Located 160 kilometres from the Pacific Ocean, the source of the Amazon, only recently discovered, was sought by explorers for centuries.
- Having searched for it for centuries, explorers recently discovered the location of the source of the Amazon, 160 kilometres from the Pacific Ocean.

5 **(Sample answer)**

The tropical Amazon is fed by torrential rains and thereby produces a fifth of the world's river water – much more than that of the longest river, the Nile. The Amazon is not only the world's widest river, owing to seasonal floods, with an average width of 8 kilometres and a depth which makes it navigable far inland, but it is also the second longest, at roughly 6300 kilometres.

8 **Any five of these:**

a Mystery: *impenetrable, inscrutable intention, gloom of overshadowed distances, you lost your way, bewitched, cut off for ever*

b Threat: *mob, unrestful and noisy, overwhelming realities, implacable force, brooding, vengeful aspect*

9 **(Sample answer)**

Passages **A** and **B** are informative non-fiction. The extract about the River Congo is fictional, literary and lyrical, i.e. its aim is to create atmosphere and evoke feelings, not to convey facts. It achieves this by using figurative language and other characteristics of descriptive writing: similes; metaphors; multiple adjectives; emotive vocabulary; alliteration; anthropomorphism (ascribing human characteristics to objects); use of the second person; reflections; repetition for effect.

10 **Facts**

- essential to support life
- covers 4% of country
- most Egyptians live on its banks
- provides water for crops and cattle
- floods every July
- 7000 kilometres long
- river mouth in Cairo
- contains crocodiles
- source discovered mid-19th century
- transport for building of pyramids
- mentioned in the Bible and literature
- used for book and film settings
- attracts tourists
- polluted by chemicals
- continuous building along banks

Fictions

- belongs to the god Isis
- pharaohs controlled it with magical powers
- inhabited by half-human, half-fish creatures
- owned by creatures who must be kept happy
- snakes created from its mud
- leisure boats have polluted it

11 **Similarities**

- very long
- floods seasonally
- contains vicious animals
- flows through jungle
- has elusive source

Differences

- Amazon carries more water
- Nile does not receive much rainfall
- different altitude
- different climate zone and vegetation
- inhabitants depend on Nile
- Nile has been literary inspiration
- Nile attracts mass tourism
- Nile is polluted
- source of Amazon discovered only recently

Unit 6

2 (Sample answers)

a raising

b labours

c provisions, board

d skill , proficiency

e valid

f sanction, condone

g struggle

h confined

3　**a** together, e.g. **connect, conflict**

　　b before, e.g. **preparation, predestined**

　　c forward, e.g. **propel, propose**

　　d across, e.g. **transmit, transitory**

　　e inside, e.g. **intravenous, introspective** (Note: **intransigent** has **in** as a negative prefix before another prefix, **trans**, and not a prefix **intra**).

　　f outside, e.g. **extravagant, extraordinary**

　　g out, e.g. **exhale, extinguish**

　　h again, e.g. **review, restore**

　　i between, e.g. **intersperse**, **intercept**

　　j within, e.g. **endanger, encircle**

4　**a** three

　　b two

　　c ten

　　d eight

　　e five

　　f two

　　g one

　　h four

　　i five

　　j eight

　　k fourteen

　　l three

　　m seven

　　n one

　　o four

　　p six

5 (Answers may include)

- the 11-year-old bull elephant called Noppakhao/Peter is an artist in Thailand who has painted a self-portrait
- has painted dozens of works over last few years of fellow elephants and natural subjects
- considered similar to Picasso in his style and use of colour
- prefers representative pictures to abstract ones
- some paintings have been sold for $700
- description of site/project/*mahout* (elephant trainer)
- description of method/tools of his painting
- meaning of his name
- character description
- quote by Asian Elephant Art & Conservation project (AEACP)

9　**a** (Sample answers)

- The moral of the story is that when one only has part of the picture, one cannot see the whole truth.
- Those who fight in the belief they are right should get together with others who have different but equally valid beliefs.
- The truth is always bigger than we can see at first.
- Human beings working alone do not arrive at the total solution.
- We are all as limited in our perception of the whole truth as a blind person.

9 b (Sample answer)

Six blind men, who were friends but competitive and who each thought they knew best, went on a trip to a zoo, where they unknowingly encountered an elephant. The six men each formed a judgement, after handling only one part of it, in turn, that it was a different object: a wall, a snake, a rope, a tree, a sword, a fan. They were arguing so much that the zookeeper heard them and arrived to recapture the elephant. The zookeeper solved the mystery by telling them that it was an elephant, and that each of them was partly right but also entirely wrong. [103 words]

Unit 7

2 (Sample answers)

a surveyed

b in complete agreement

c deep

d hazardous, dangerous

e exposed

f integral, essential

g future generations

h irreversibly

i deconstruct, take to pieces

j reducing, decreasing

3 a reunited

b removed

c reciprocal

d resist

e restitution

f rewound

g relocation

h repatriation

i retrograde

j resources

4 For a completed and dated action in the past we use the **past simple**, whereas for an action which began in the past but which is not yet completed, we use the **present perfect**. The past perfect tense is used when an action **occurred before another action in the past**. The past continuous shows that an action **was already occurring** when **another action interrupted it**.

5 a I visited the exhibition, which I heard about on the radio.

b I read about the man who had stolen the statues.

c I bought a book which was about the history of Greece.

d I met Lord Byron, who had written a poem the previous day.

e We have not visited Greece, which we have heard is a beautiful country.

f I spoke to a woman in the gallery who(m) I had met previously.

g It is difficult to find the people who are responsible for the damage.

h This is the Museum Director, who is against the return of the marbles.

i They didn't find the sculpture(,) which was buried by an earthquake.

j You should have interviewed Lord Elgin, who(m) I introduced to you.

6 a 100%.

b They were loaded on board ships to take them to Britain, and one of the ships sank.

c The Tasmanians.

d Removal, pollution, cleaning.

e Disapproval of their having been stolen (e.g. Lord Byron denounced Elgin as a vandal); celebration of them as works of art – John Keats saw them exhibited in London and was inspired to write two sonnets about them.

7   **(Answers may include)**
- an argument supporting the Greek claim to the marbles
- the British Museum's rationale for retaining them
- explanation of what the marbles consist of (e.g. why they are important)
- history of the marbles
- description of attempts to remove them
- case for their return to Greece
- previous reasons for not returning them
- implications for future of museum property.

11   **a** into   **c** to   **e** on (about)   **g** of
     b about   **d** of   **f** from

12   High water is most likely to occur between September and April, though it's not unheard of at other times. July is just about the only dry month in a city of water built in a lagoon in the Adriatic Sea. If you are a tourist planning ahead, you can expect the highest tides around the time of a full moon, or a new moon. When a level above 110 centimetres is expected – which will invade nearly 12% of Venice – sirens will sound a warning three–four hours in advance of high tide, with an increasing number of tones to signify every 10 centimetres above 110 centimetres, warning residents to protect their properties and get out their wellington boots. The speakers are concealed inside bell towers and public buildings.

     For half a century, there has been constant debate on how to save the city, but no agreement can be reached, not even on whether the situation is getting worse. The number of high tides varies between 80 and 100 in consecutive years, without any apparent trend; the worst flood of 194 centimetres was in 1966, but in 2001, there was a high tide of 144 centimetres. What is certain is that the Adriatic has risen by 23 centimetres over the last 50 years, after decades of stability. This may be due to global factors, or to heavy draining of underground water by local factories; an aggravating factor is that the city also suffers from subsidence.

13   **a** Vocabulary and imagery suggest attack – *fears, threatens, danger, overwhelm, relentless, eating into*
         Emotive language evokes pity – *drowning home, schoolchildren.*
         Priceless conveys the irreplaceable loss of the art treasures.
         The use of statistics shows how real the threat is – *the population has dwindled by 100 000 in 50 years to 70 000; 80 centimetres; $5 million; 50 times a year, 12% of Venice.*
         The giant cruise vessels sound threateningly large and incongruous with canals and fragile architecture.
     b *Unpredictability* means that Venetians cannot be properly prepared for the high tides.
         Uncertainty and disagreement make finding a solution difficult – *constant debate, no agreement, without any apparent trend, half a century.*
         The *aggravating factor* of subsidence makes matters seem worse.
         The *additional cause of damage* is yet another problem to be resolved.

14   **(Sample answer)**
- Afraid city will be drowned
- Buldings being destroyed
- Venetians forced to leave city / move to higher floors etc.
- Unsure when the next high water will come.

- Fear for children's safety.
- Historic buildings and art treasures being damaged.
- Visitors and students put off coming to city.
- Sea continues to rise; no adequate protection.
- Residents matter more than cruisers.
- City in danger of being washed away.
- Authorities must agree on and implement measures regardless of cost.

Unit 8

2   1. However 2. Nonetheless 3. Consequently 4. Unfortunately 5. Nevertheless 6. In addition 7. Moreover

3   replicate – replica; epitomised – epitome; catastrophically – catastrophe; denying – denial; defying – defiance

4   commodities – products; ensued – followed; disabused – disillusioned, enlightened, undeceived; Notwithstanding – despite, regardless of; remains – bodies, corpses

5   *in tandem with* – metaphor; more unusual/interesting way of saying together with
denying national frontiers and defying territorial boundaries – parallel structure of verbal noun, adjective, noun; an elegant phrase with alliteration and assonance
the balloon dream deflated – pun plus alliteration, poetic effect
wiped out – strong phrasal verb, metaphorical
Going with the wind – play on words (Gone with the Wind is a classic book/film title), comic effect

6   **a** Ways in which hot air ballooning has failed to live up to expectations:
   – dangerous; deaths and accidents
   – not future of travel
   – not a weapon of war
   b Ways in which hot air ballooning has continued to be appealing:
   – form of entertainment
   – research tool
   – challenge
   – freedom / no engine

9   **a** Informal vocab and syntax: simple and monosyllabic words; repeated words; contractions; abbreviations; redundancies, idioms; clichés; simple and compound sentences; sentences beginning with But; missing appositional commas
   b News report structure: news fact at the beginning, followed by background/lead-up and details plus inclusion of quotations, finishing with looking to the future

10 **a** At the time; When; After; For the next 4 days; Six months later; By the time; Shortly after; Currently
   b They are not strictly necessary to the story, but they give a chronological structure to the narrative; they link the events; they give information about duration; they avoid the use of 'then'. (Notice that they are not duplicated.)

129

11   She accepted the proposal. (10)   They plan to get married the following year. (12)
     He lost his wallet. (1)   He visited her at work. (4)
     They met in a shop. (2)   He climbed the bridge. (7)
     She gave him a free curry. (3)   He was caught by security. (6)
     He went to Fukushima. (5)   He sent her a photo. (9)
     They went to Bali. (8)   They got engaged. (11)

12   I met Keow in May 2016 in Japan, while he was there to take photos of the melt-down at Fukushima. After he lost his wallet containing a large amount of money, he came into the food store where I was working. I was pleased to discover he spoke English, which I also know because I learned it in Poland. He seemed shy and distant at first - I think he assumed I already had a boyfriend - but then he asked for my phone number.

Six months later I was sitting in a restaurant while on holiday in Bali. While Keow went to the bathroom, I checked my phone and found a photo and message saying 'Will you marry me'. I discovered later that his proposal came from the top of the tallest bridge in China. I posted the answer 'Yes' and burst into tears. Afterwards we went to Kuta beach and he put an engagement ring on my finger. We're getting married next year and will settle in Malaysia when I've finished my studies in Japan.

Unit 9

3   **a** malfunctions   **b** unwieldy   **c** advent   **d** overzealous   **e** orientation

4   **a** cracks and fissures; anaconda's embrace
    b nooks and crannies; unfathomable

5   **a** *madness*; *horrifyingly claustrophobic*; *an anaconda's embrace*
    b *insane*; *horrible side effects*; *the bends are bad*
    c The writer does not understand why anyone would want to take part in these highly unpleasant and dangerous activities.

6   Dangers of cave exploration – narrow cracks, dark holes, tight tunnels, claustrophobia, panic, unrealistic aims, losing sense of direction.
    Dangers of deep-water diving – poisonous oxygen, falling asleep, wrong air mix, nausea, amnesia, fits, the bends, shallow breathing, faulty equipment, running out of air, poor visibility.

7   **(Sample answer)**
    Cave-diving
    This activity combines the exploration of caves and potholes with underwater diving. Both are considered to be dangerous sports, and the combination makes cave-diving much more so because of the possibility of becoming trapped, running out of air or suffering the side effects of poisonous air, and because of the necessity for precise timing. The main hazard is loss of orientation, causing the explorer to travel in the wrong direction. Divers must resurface slowly from a great depth in order to avoid damage to the body. Unlike in other extreme sports, a rush of adrenalin is not advantageous or enjoyable, as it is a requirement for safety to stay relaxed and not to panic. When the sport first began, without the benefit of technical aids and using heavy and awkward diving suits, there were many accidents. The use of a guideline is still considered to be a sensible precaution.

9   **a**   *sole*; *dense*; *tremendous*; *intense*; *paralysing*; *single*; *gigantic*; *astonishing*; *immense*; *profound*; *dizzying*; *fearsome*

   b   *seized, smashed, rammed* – These verbs convey the violence of the attack on the ship and the the apparently deliberate damage inflicted by a heavy vessel.

   c   *monster, beast, creature* – These nouns imply that they were attacked by a huge, hostile and horrific animal.

10   **(Examples of suitable points)**
   fading lights, set in late evening, nearly drowns twice, attack by a vicious *monster*; ship unable to return, long wait, darkness descends, exhaustion and loss of voice (to show helplessness), use of ellipses (to show loss of control), an unknown *something* and *it* (only later turns into *someone* and reader assumes it is the monster); cry for help; frequent use of exclamations (to show fear and amazement); discovery that 'gigantic whale' is made of impermeable steel (making it both unnatural and indestructible); use of triplet (*This animal, this monster, this natural phenomenon*); sudden spurt of speed and fear of falling off; uniformity of the 'beast' (suggesting military capability); disappearance of the moon; reference to 'whatever beings' (suggesting non-humans); unnatural silence of the eight men; suddenness and efficiency of the 'capture', being imprisoned; the unknown fate awaiting the three (outnumbered) captives; the fearful question 'With whom were we dealing?'

11   An hour later, I was overcome with tremendous exhaustion. My limbs stiffened in the grip of intense cramps and paralysing cold. I tried to call out. My swollen lips wouldn't let a single sound through. I heard my friend cry 'Help!'. Ceasing all movement for an instant, we listened. His shout had received an answer. I could barely hear it. I was at the end of my strength; my fingers gave out; my mouth opened convulsively, filling with brine … // Just then something hard banged against me. I clung to it and was pulled back to the surface. I fainted … then someone was shaking me vigorously. // 'Ned!' I exclaimed. 'You were thrown overboard after the collision?' // 'Yes, professor, but I was luckier than you and immediately able to set foot on our gigantic whale. I soon realized why my harpoon got blunted and couldn't puncture its hide. This beast is made of plated steel!'

12   The professor seems an exuberant character, judging from his use of exclamations. He is sensible enough to realise they might need to wait a long time, and that they should conserve their energy; he decides how best to do it, and makes the necessary calculation, evidence that he is educated and used to being in charge. He is able to appreciate the beauty of the sea at night, even in his desperate situation. His physical state seems less robust than that of the other swimmers, as he loses his strength and succumbs to exhaustion. His analysis of the 'carapace' of the 'creature' is scientific and uses technical language; his deductions lead him to arrive at a conclusive judgement that they were dealing with an 'immense steel fish'. He is used to being precise in his observations, giving 80 centimetres as the distance the 'fish' was protruding from the surface.

13   Points to be included:
   fell overboard as a result of the impact of a supposed whale attack on the *Abraham Lincoln* at 11 p.m.; found his friend in the water; shared swimming with him for an hour; became too weak and too cold to continue; lost his voice; mouth filled with seawater; started to lose consciousness and drown; returned to surface by holding on to something; was brought round by a sailor called 'Ned' who explained that it wasn't really a whale; climbed on top and investigated what it was made of; had to hold on tight when the submarine picked up speed; buffeted by waves; at dawn, eight men came out of the machine and quickly took professor and companions down into it.

Unit 10

2   (Sample answers)

   a The effect of the title is to make the reader expect it to be about an enemy attack.

   b The words in bold have connotations of serious crime and mortal danger.

   c The underlined words in the passage create a sustained metaphor of mosquitoes and humans being enemies engaged in battle.

   d The rhetorical questions, imperative sentences and non-sentences add a sense of drama and urgency to the passage.

   e The use of *we* makes the assumption that the reader has had the same experiences and shares the writer's hostile feelings towards mosquitoes

3   a *raise* is a regular transitive verb (requiring an object) meaning to put something in a higher position, e.g. *He raised his head*

      rise is an irregular intransitive verb meaning to put oneself

      in a higher position, e.g. *He rose from his bed*

      arise is an irregular intransitive verb meaning

      to occur, e.g. *An unforeseen problem arose.*

   b raise – raised – raised; rise – rose – risen; arise – arose – arisen.

5 The first conditional uses the **present simple** tense with the future tense for events which are **probable**. Second conditionals, which use the simple past followed by **would** plus **the infinitive (without to)**, signify an event which could happen but which is **improbable**. Third conditionals, formed with the **past perfect** tense followed by **would have** plus **the past participle**, mean that the event is **impossible** because it **is too late**. There are also zero conditionals, using simple present in both clauses, which refer to **permanent truths**.

6   (Sample answers)

   Air-borne invaders; The invincible enemy; Evil monsters; The invisible menace

7   (Sample answers)

a	we are not aware of them until too late	**f**	we have to waste time dealing with them
b	the noise they make gives the impression of celebrating victory	**g**	we have to make an effort to deal with them
c	they behave sneakily	**h**	it costs money to deal with them
d	they bite/leave a painful swelling	**i**	they steal our blood
e	they spread malaria	**j**	they are very difficult to kill

8   (Answers may include)

   • Mosquitoes are a carrier of a deadly disease which affects many parts of the world.

   • Without protection, you may contract malaria, which can be fatal.

   • The insects are small and may not be easily visible, so always be vigilant.

   • Listen for the characteristic buzzing sound they make while flying.

   • Keep all parts of your body covered when mosquitoes may be present.

- Sprays, coils, creams or nets should be used before settling to sleep at night.
- In some cases it may be advisable to take anti-malarial pills.
- Areas of standing water near your home should be drained or sprayed.

10 **(Sample answers)**
preternaturally – inexplicably, abnormally; *perseveringly* – determinedly, persistently, tenaciously; *convulsively* – jerkily, twitchily; *vexation* – annoyance, irritation; *diverting* – distracting; *forebodings* – apprehensions, premonitions, omens, misgivings; *unwholesome* – unhealthy, harmful; *adorned* – decorated, furnished; *ruffian* – lout, hooligan; *astronomer* – scientific observer of the stars

11 setting – unknown room, four-poster bed, water dripping, dark old picture.
atmosphere – stifling, unwholesome; persona is nervous, wide awake, feverish, wondering; the repetition of *now* and list of futile actions in the first paragraph convey inability to sleep and expectation that something unpleasant will happen.
language – *groaned, horrors, rack, forebodings, danger, suffering, terror, shading, intently, constraint, gloomy, sinister ruffian; desperado.*

12 **(Sample answers)**
a   After having realised he would not be able to sleep, the narrator looked around the room.
b   Before noticing the picture, the narrator studied the furniture.
c   Not only could the narrator not sleep, but he was also frightened.
d   Even though he tried his pillow in several positions, he could not find a comfortable one.
e   In spite of the moonlight and the candle glow, the narrator could not see the picture clearly.

133

Unit 11

2 **(Sample answers)**

a   moving fast
b   favoured with
c   disadvantaged by
d   from the beginning
e   going towards
f   more than
g   say no to
h   difficult to improve on

4 **(Sample answer)**

The world-renowned IceHotel is a completely new experience in holiday travel and accommodation. Not only is the beauty of the snowy Scandinavian landscape all around you, with its unique winter sports, but you get the experience of actually living in it. Yes, the Ice Hotel is actually made of ice, and so are many of the things in it. But no, it isn't cold! The world's largest frozen palace is cosy and welcoming, and all the thermal wear you need is provided.

After a day being driven in a sledge pulled by huskies, or cross-country skiing – or even lassoing reindeer – you can return to the warmth of your fur-covered ice bed. If you prefer, you can take a snowmobile and overnight in a wilderness cabin with steaming sauna.

Every winter the hotel is built again, so it's always new.

You'll have plenty of tales to tell your friends when you get home!

7 **(Some examples of suitable sentences)**

- After waking up from a deep sleep – because by night-time I feel so exhausted owing to the continual work and the effect of the cold – we had a long meeting about the expedition in which we organised our food rations for the weeks ahead.
- Despite our breakfast consisting of granola and oats, lunch of carbohydrate bars, soup and nuts, and dinner of pasta or rice, we also somehow have to eat a block of butter a day to keep our energy levels up.
- This afternoon I went to build an igloo with Simon, one of the three Inuit hunters with our party, who is great because he's got a true sense of humour and I feel safer having him around, since he knows the environment well, having killed his first polar bear when he was six.

8 **(Sample answer)**

Questions, exclamations and direct speech convey the drama of the situation and Sam's panic. (Polar bears have already been mentioned on 23rd April as something to cause *frissons of fear*.) The action is interspersed with description of the bear to slow the narrative pace; mist and light are mentioned to create mysteriousness, as if the bear has supernatural power; short paragraphs convey the idea of events happening quickly and out of control; live ammunition is referred to, and even the cracker shells are enough to kill a person; the bear is moving aggressively towards them *(charged) with real purpose*. The fact that the bear was hungry, didn't scare easily, and was as big as they get – a full-grown male bear – all add to the threat posed by the animal.

9 **(Sample answers)**

- Was the temperature a problem?
- Did you feel lonely?
- What was your most frightening experience on the trip?
- What was the food like?
- Did you have local Inuits with the party?
- What was your best experience on the trip?
- What are the dangers of trekking across snowy landscape?
- How has global warming affected the Arctic?

11 **(Sample answer)**

a Sam enjoyed the peacefulness of the place, the beautiful scenery and the magnificent wild life, as well as the company and skills of the Inuit.

b He was concerned about the effects of global warming in the area, which include a high rate of UV radiation, the melting ice, hungry animals (because of the population decline of the prey and increased competition among predatory species), and the threat to both the livelihood of the Inuit hunters and to the planet as a whole.

Unit 12

2 **a** *psychic awareness* – telepathic/supernatural realisation
genetic code – biochemical rules within living cells which determine protein building
nature and nurture – heredity and environment

   b What do the prefixes on the following words mean?
interviewed – between; extrovert – outside; introvert – inside; confusion – together;
reflective – again; perception – through; encompass – around; simultaneously – together, same

3 po<u>ss</u>ess; h<u>eigh</u>tened; g<u>uar</u>anteed; a<u>ckn</u>owle<u>dg</u>es; <u>wrest</u>led

4 Examples of other speech verbs: considers, agrees, confirms, rejoins, suggests, points out, remarks

5 **a** Effect of the use of direct speech:
The voices of the twins dominate the passage; they are the focus of the passage/research;
their personalities (and their similarities) are conveyed; the researcher is only the facilitator and
has the lowest possible profile; it seems more like a dialogue than an interview.

6 **a** impact – marked effect;   **b** intimacy – closeness;
   c affinity – rapport, empathy;   **d** polarisation – division into opposing positions;
   e entity – independent existence

7 **(Sample answer)**
Being a twin is the most intimate relationship there is, and even includes telepathic communication.
No other relationship can compete with that between twins or live up to their expectations. Twins feel
both more connected than non-twins, because everything is shared between them, but also more
isolated from the rest of the world, People treat them as a double entity and sometimes view them
negatively. Twins have to reflect more on their identity and how to define it than most people, as they
want to be seen as individuals leading separate lives. (92 words)

10 **a** There is a small group of usually two-syllabled words which have a slightly different spelling for
the **verb** form and the **noun** form. We spell the word with an *s* when we are referring to the **verb**,
but with a *c* when we are using the **noun**.
(NB American English use of 's' and 'c' in these words is different.)

   b enrol, patrol, extol; refer, prefer; emit, omit, permit, submit, admit
Note also travel – travelling; jewel – jewellery; pedal – pedalling
(NB American English does not double the consonant in the last four and other similar cases.)

   c preferred, offering, transference, reference, referral, deterrent, installs, benefitted

11 Give synonyms for the following words as used in Passage **B**.
accords – corresponds, agrees, tallies, matches
immaterial – irrelevant, unimportant, insignificant
anomaly – oddity, peculiarity, abnormality, irregularity
concentration – close/dense gathering, cluster
prohibitive – restrictive, excessive, exorbitant, impossible

135

12 **a** Facts relating to the birth of twins in Kodinhi:
   six times higher than global average
   220 produced by 2000 inhabitants / 10% of town's population
   45 twin births in 1000 / 4.5%
   rest of India has rate of 4% / 0.4%
   In 2008, 15 pairs born of 300 healthy deliveries
   60 pairs born in last 5 years
   rate is increasing year-on-year
   majority identical
   number of twins has doubled in 10 years
   phenomenon started in 1949
   the local school has 30-40 sets of twins at any one time

   b Theories relating to the birth of twins generally:
   diet may be the cause
   tropical yams could be relevant
   a pollutant can be to blame
   IVF is known to increase twin rate
   mature women more likely to have twins
   women over 5 ft 3 inches (160.02cm) more likely to have twins
   women's partners not a factor
   the Theories relating to the birth of twins generally

13 Experts have been unable to find a (1) **solution** to the mystery of what has been (2) **dubbed/ named/called** the Twin Town of India, where a (3) **record/abnormal/extraordinary** number of twin births has become a (4) **repeated/regular** phenomenon, and one which is inexplicable. The local doctor is (5) **convinced/anxious/determined** that there should be research done to (6) **determine/discover/establish** the cause, so that the findings can be applied to fertility treatments. None of the theories which have been (7) **considered/espoused/expressed** are relevant to this case so far, but the doctor believes that diet may prove to be a (8) **factor/ decisive/crucial/relevant**. In the meantime, the experts continue to be (9) **perplexed/baffled/ stumped** and the twins continue to enjoy being able to (10) **deceive/confuse/trick** their teachers and neighbours.